The CITIZEN POETS *of* Boston

The CITIZEN POETS *of* Boston

A COLLECTION OF FORGOTTEN POEMS, 1789–1820

PAUL LEWIS, *Editor*

UNIVERSITY PRESS OF NEW ENGLAND *Hanover and London*

University Press of New England
www.upne.com
© 2016 University Press of New England
All rights reserved
Manufactured in the United States of America
Designed by Richard Hendel
Typeset in Arnhem by Passumpsic Publishing

For permission to reproduce any of the material in this book,
contact Permissions, University Press of New England, One Court Street,
Suite 250, Lebanon NH 03766; or visit www.upne.com

Library of Congress Cataloging-in-Publication Data
The citizen poets of Boston: a collection of forgotten poems,
1789–1820 / Paul Lewis, editor.
    pages cm
Includes bibliographical references.
ISBN 978-1-61168-887-0 (cloth: alk. paper)—
ISBN 978-1-61168-888-7 (pbk.: alk. paper)—
ISBN 978-1-61168-930-3 (ebook)
1. American poetry—Massachusetts—Boston.
2. American poetry—18th century. 3. American poetry—
19th century. I. Lewis, Paul, 1949– editor.
PS549.B6C58 2016
811.008'0974461—dc232015031966

5 4 3 2 1

Frontispiece: *Boston, from City Point near Sea Street*, 1808
Courtesy of the Boston Public Library, Print Department

To the members of the citizen poets research team—Sean Cahill,

Kristin L. Canfield, Jaimie Carvalho, Nicholas Clements, Kelsie Dorn,

Jennifer Fuksman, Elizabeth Gavin, Caroline M. Kirkwood, Kristen House,

Michael Kadow, Harrison Kent, Alexandra Mitropoulos, Erica Navarro,

Elizabeth M. Powers, Tracy Rizk, Meidema Sanchez, and

Nicholas A. Volpe—

and

to the unknown author of "The Poet"

for proving that poets neither "hold talk" with Philomel

nor "live in castles made of air."

CONTENTS

PREFACE

What constitutes American literature has grown exponentially in recent decades, first in response to critical outcries about neglected groups of writers—including women, African Americans, and devout Christians—and then in response to online access to long-forgotten texts. Until recently, finding rarely or never republished work that appeared in American newspapers and magazines before the Civil War was a daunting task. No physical archive held all the extant publications. Even if such a collection had been housed in a single place, searching it to find work on specific topics or in specific genres would have required a lifetime of effort.

The expansion of American literature advanced at what might have seemed a rapid rate during the 1980s when standard anthologies began to move beyond the established canon of familiar classics. But it took the creation of online archives—like the HathiTrust, Archive of Americana, and American Periodical Series—to enhance opportunities for cultural archaeology, exploration, and exhumation in literary study. Empowered by technology, researchers can now access most of the work published in American magazines within specific genres, particular cities, or specific date ranges.

This book is the product of one such effort in which Boston College students, working in small groups over three years, reviewed thousands of poems that were published in Boston magazines between 1789 and 1820. We began in 1789 because we wanted to focus on Boston as a city in the new nation and because the first magazines that seemed promising, the *Gentlemen and Ladies' Town and Country Magazine* and the *Massachusetts Magazine*, date from this time. We stopped in 1820 because, in the following decade, more poems were published in Boston magazines than in the three decades covered in this volume. Moreover, during the 1820s and in succeeding decades, as interstate commerce grew, American poets were less likely to be writing for local audiences. Within our time frame, the poems we considered introduced us to a generation of Bostonians who invited us into their homes, engaged us in conversations, and opened doors to the life of the city two hundred years ago. Over and over, in the work of mostly anonymous and long-forgotten poets, we heard Old Boston singing. We think that, as you turn these pages, you will too.

A NOTE ON SPELLING, PUNCTUATION, CAPITALIZATION, AND NOTES

To reflect the dynamism of both language and printing in the early national period, poems appear with their original spelling. In this way, one poem uses older or English spellings (for instance, "musick," "honour," "blest," and "tho'") while another uses newer or American versions (for instance, "music," "honor," "blessed," or "though"). Archaic but still-familiar pronouns (for instance, "ye," "thee," "thy," "thou," and "thine") appear in some of the poems, while modern forms appear in others. Similarly, the use of "'d" at the end of verbs has been preserved where found, or "preserv'd" as some of these texts would have it. If a poem originally featured the same words—for instance, *won't* and *wont* or *Christian* and *christian*—in different forms, that is how it appears here.

During the early national period, poem titles used a dizzying array of lettering, including large and small capitals in every combination of italics and regular fonts. Except in the table of contents, these titles appear in their original forms.

A few potentially distracting practices have been modernized and standardized. Long or medial s's (which could appear as "ſ" or "f" in the poems) have been changed to short s's. Punctuation marks that appear a space or more after the word they follow, a common practice at the time, have been moved left, next to the last letter of the word. Ellipses, which could consist of any number of periods, appear as three spaced dots (. . .), and dashes, which appeared as either one or any number of spaced lines with varying lengths, appear here as em-dashes (—). When dashes were used redundantly in combination with other punctuation marks (for instance, ;—), only one of these marks made it into the versions here. Single and double quotation marks, which were used in various ways, have been modernized in the interest of clearly delineating where speeches and quotations begin and end. Our editorial notes are identified with daggers in the lines of the poems. Explanatory notes that appeared in the original texts are identified with asterisks; the corresponding notes include the words "original note" in brackets.

The CITIZEN POETS *of* Boston

INTRODUCTION

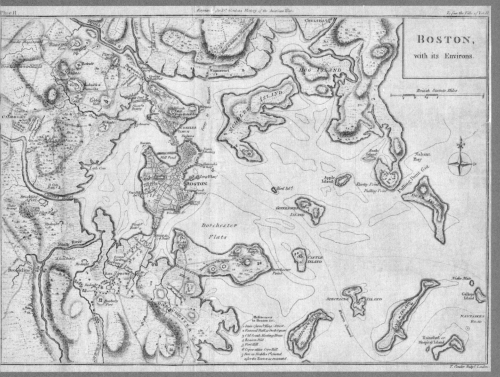

Boston, with its Environs. Map. Engraving by T. Conder, Sculpt. (London : s.n., 1788). Massachusetts Historical Society

Messrs. Gilbert & Dean, IF you think the [enclosed poem], occasioned by reading . . . your 29th number, will answer for a Supplement, you perhaps will publish it, when you have nothing better. If it be not so fortunate as to "excite a smile," it may shew some of your fair readers "their own image."
— Headnote written by the poet and included with "Here comes Miss LIGHTHEAD and her tasty sister," which appeared in the *Boston Weekly Magazine* on June 11, 1803

Whether I shall be, or not,
A poet up to Walter Scott;
Or whether I've right to hope
To write like Byron, Swift, or Pope; . . .
Admits no doubt—I'll tell you why;
Because, forsooth, I ne'er shall try.
— Anonymous, "*AN EPISTLE* TO THE EDITOR," *Ladies' Port Folio*, April 22, 1820

Everything published among us must have some value, . . . as affording insight into the spirit and temper of the times.
— Samuel Kettell, "Preface," *Specimens of American Poetry*, 1829

In 1789 there were a few ways to get to Boston. You could arrive by ship or ferry. You could traverse the three-year-old bridge that ran from Charlestown to the North End. Or you could walk or ride over Boston Neck, the thin strip of land that linked the island-like city to the mainland of Massachusetts. Imagine that you have come this way, perhaps on horseback from the rural community of Roxbury, and that you are now trotting along the recently renamed Washington Street past farms and fields toward the spires of the Old South Meeting House and the Old North Church. Approaching the center of town, you smell sea salt from the harbor and cow dung from the Common. The further you go on the streets of Old Boston, the more entranced you are by the sights and sounds of everyday life: mechanics at work, clerks opening shops, men rushing on business, women shaking out mats and chasing chickens, children hurrying to school, carts and carriages bustling everywhere.

By recovering rarely or never reprinted poems published in Boston magazines during the early national period (1789–1820), this book bridges the gap between twenty-first-century readers and the post-Revolutionary city.

The team that compiled it, composed of the editor and Boston College English majors, invites you to regard the poems we have exhumed, enjoyed, and selected as buckboard time machines. Because most of them were published anonymously by amateur or citizen poets, and because they tend to be unpretentious, informal, and even conversational, they can seem intimate, revealing, and alive. Divided into groups organized around particular subjects and arranged in chronological order, they allow us to eavesdrop on diners swapping stories at a late-eighteenth-century tavern, overhear a conversation between clerks and customers in a sewing shop, get stuck in a traffic jam in Charlestown, join a crowd of people rushing to see a fire, sit down at a Thanksgiving feast fifty-nine years before Thanksgiving became an official American holiday, watch Harvard students wait for the results of their examinations, try to solve a riddle that has gone unsolved for 217 years, share a parent's concern about what life will bring a sleeping daughter, meet a young woman determined not to be dominated by a future husband, and enjoy arch comments about husbands, wives, sons, daughters, doctors, lawyers, politicians, ministers, and poets.

During the early national period, no fewer than 427 magazines were published in a country new enough to be referred to as "these United States." Astonishingly, these often fledging periodicals included over 30,000 poems in their pages. In Boston alone—between 1789, when the *Massachusetts Magazine* began its seven-year run on old Newbury Street, and 1820, when the *Ladies' Port Folio* began its five-month run on State Street—at least 59 magazines contained over 4,500 poems. The sheer volume of verse that appeared in the United States during these decades partially explains our focus on Boston magazines. It's one thing to review more than 4,500 poems, quite another to review more than 30,000. Beyond this, concentrating on poems written for readers in and near a specific city responds to the geographically limited distribution of magazines in this period. As Frank Luther Mott, a historian of the American magazine, notes, publishing in these decades was "for the most part local . . . supported by contributions of local coteries and by subscriptions drawn chiefly from within a radius of fifty miles." Projects like this need to have a local focus, to be driven, as this one was, by the desire to know more about the place where one lives, works, or studies. If teachers and students in other parts of the country—such as New York City and Philadelphia, where research may be particularly fruitful—undertake similar explorations, they will, we predict, make similarly delightful discoveries that they can then share, as we are doing now, with interested readers in their cities.[1]

While the number of poems published during these years seems large, literary historians have noted and our electronic searches confirm that most of the verse printed in these magazines was reprinted from British periodicals and books. Lacking both financial and authorial capital, the editors of these fledging publications took advantage of the extremely limited domestic protection for authors and the absence of an international copyright to pirate works, often failing to identify the names of sources and writers. At the same time, these editors frequently invited submissions by their own readers, some of whom eagerly responded by submitting poems. Works by these mostly anonymous reader or citizen poets are heavily represented in each subject-based section of this anthology.[2]

As used here, the word *citizen* refers not to residents who enjoyed full rights and privileges but to residents in general, who, if they were so inclined, could attempt to participate in the give-and-take of Boston's nascent literary culture. Members of groups denied equal treatment—including women, people of color, young adults, and people who didn't own property—could submit poems for consideration. We know, for example, that two poets who published in Boston under their own names either during or just before this period—Phillis Wheatley (1753–84), an enslaved woman, and David Hitchcock (1773–?), a shoemaker—fit into one or more of these categories. Though most of the poets included here were undoubtedly European Americans, and though many were obviously well read, anonymous publication makes it impossible in most cases to determine their gender, race, and class. While this lack of certainty about authors can be frustrating, it can also create opportunities for imaginative reading as elements of style, voice, or theme provide intimations of identity.

The word *magazines* also requires an explanation insofar as the earlier a publication's run, the more likely that it would have included not only literary genres but also news and commentary. Indeed, the hybrid nature of these periodicals extended into the stories and poems they featured. Fiction and poetry frequently engaged the same current issues as the essays and news features, and writers frequently crossed genre lines by combining fiction, nonfiction, and verse in a single work. For instance, the September 1794 issue of the *Massachusetts Magazine* contains both an essay by Judith Sargent Murray (1751–1820) on the treatment of religion in post-revolutionary France and an anonymous poem, possibly also by Murray. The essay begins with an original verse epigraph and uses brief narratives and personal reflections to support its defense of the moral value of benevolent religion; the poem uses images and ideas associated with the French Revolution to promote woman's equality and liberation. Beyond this, published poems were used for a range of what we would now consider highly unpoetic purposes, including advertisements, letters, arguments, and even prospectuses for the magazines.

Many of these poems have eluded detection and analysis for several reasons. First, it has until recently been difficult to find and study magazines scattered in distant archives. Second, even when found, it has been impossible in many cases to distinguish native from imported work. Third, the way poems appear in what often seem crude publications—tumbled in with tide reports, death notices, advertisements, fiction, and nonfiction—deprives them of the elevated standing often granted to poetry. Fourth, they lack formal variety. And fifth, the practice of publishing anonymously means that readers have been unable to associate most of this work with specific writers, so each poem has stood on its own—or, rather, fallen in most cases into obscurity.

In the interest of full disclosure, it's necessary to concede that historians of American magazines have offered critical, or at best mixed, assessments of poetry published during the early national period. Lyon N. Richardson notes that the first volume of the *Massachusetts Magazine* (in 1789) featured "original poetry" by "persons who . . . [lacked] creative power and the higher associative qualities of the mind." Mott, who studied American magazines published between 1741 and 1930, emphasized the preference among late eighteenth- and early nineteenth-century American readers for classic and contemporary British writers, including Milton, Shakespeare, Pope, Wordsworth, Coleridge, Byron, and especially Scott. And Mott concluded that "in verse the period was deficient, so far as America is concerned." Mott's view has been echoed or implicitly assumed even by more recent critics who see the cultural significance of the first magazines published in the United States. In a study of American magazines published between 1810 and 1820, Neal L. Edgar regards the search for American poetry in this decade as "unrewarding," insofar as "original poetry for the magazines was not done by skillful hands." About work published in the *Massachusetts Magazine* (1789–96), Edward E. Chielens dismissively observes that "the bulk of poetry . . . is sentimental and didactic." Jared Gardner, whose study *The Rise and Fall of Early American Magazine Culture* describes and celebrates the genre-crossing combinations of fiction and nonfiction in these periodicals, pays no attention whatsoever to the poems that regularly appeared alongside and within the prose, thus intensifyng the hybrid effect. And it's worth noting that the Library of America's volume of *American Poetry: The Seventeenth and*

Eighteenth Centuries includes only nine anonymously published poems, a tiny fraction of the number of poems published in this way. This is particularly unfortunate given that anonymous and pseudonymous publication opened these magazines to female writers who were excluded from other forms of public expression.[3]

Taking such factors into account, we approached these long-disparaged and neglected poems with a narrow mission. Reading only magazines published in Boston, we waded through many imitative, flat, formal, or amateurish poems in search of buried treasures: poems that somehow provide a glimpse of the felt life of this place at specific moments in its early history as an American city. While the critics who disparaged the poems in our first literary magazines were mostly correct in describing the bulk of them as awkward, mawkish, posing, or self-consciously "poetic," here and there, as you are about to see, we found works that captured the texture of life—what people were doing, thinking, and feeling—in the city. With so much of the early architecture of Boston ravaged by fire, the poems selected for inclusion here allow one to see the place through the eyes of its citizen poets.

Recovering these poems and choosing which to include has, then, been a project of literary archaeology. The task required us to consider why some poems survive and others don't, what makes a poem "good" and what poems are "good for." Like the author of "Here comes Miss LIGHT-HEAD and her tasty sister"—included in the June 11, 1803, issue of the *Boston Weekly Magazine*—we came to treasure poems that hold mirrors up to the world in which they were created, conveying what Samuel Kettell, an early collector of American verse, called "the spirit of the times." Like the anonymous author of "*AN EPISTLE* TO THE EDITOR" that ran in the April 22, 1820, issue of the *Ladies' Port Folio*, we celebrate the straightforward, unpretentious directness of the poems collected here. At times opinionated, at times amused or mournful, Boston's citizen poets exude a becoming modesty, a sense that they are writing not for the ages but for and about friends, relatives, and fellow citizens, that they drew inspiration not from the muses but from the lives they were living. Declaring that he will never attempt to reach the heights of famous British or classic poetry, the speaker in "*AN EPISTLE* TO THE EDITOR" is happy to aim lower:

> But now and then, in leisure time,
> For sport, I try my hand at rhyme,
> And send on to your Ladies' Folio,
> To eke out your poetic Olio.

Some specimens I here enclose,
O'er which your patrons kind may doze,
Calmly, as though they were in prose.

In a similarly self-effacing mood, the anonymous author of "To the memory of William Holbrook, Milton," which ran in the September 1794 issue of the *Massachusetts Magazine*, addressed a note to the editors that they then published along with the poem: "As the author of the following lines very seldom attempts poetical writings, imperfections will be more excusable."

Two, perhaps conflicting, qualities of the poems published in Boston during these years stand out in the illustration and epigraph used in the first issues of the *Boston Weekly Magazine* in 1802.

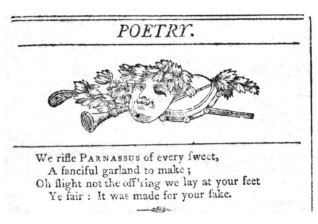

POETRY.

We rifle PARNASSUS of every sweet,
A fanciful garland to make;
Oh flight not the off'ring we lay at your feet
Ye fair : It was made for your fake.

On the one hand, the image—with its mask, garland, horn, drum, and rifle—pretentiously evokes classical mythology, military swagger, and general artsiness: highbrow impressions underscored by the reference to Mount Parnassus, home of the muses. On the other hand, the word "rifle" (used ironically in the sense of a harmless kind of robbery or as a comic deflation of military plunder) brings this characterization down from the mountain to the realm of mortals. Similarly, the defensiveness of "Oh slight not the off'ring we lay at your feet" leads into the direct and seemingly personal address of "Ye fair: it was made for your sake." In choosing poems for this collection, we tended to put aside pretenders to high art, invokers of the muses, and deployers of flowery language in favor of work that established a direct connection between the writer's experience, thought, or feelings and the reader.

The migration of these long-neglected publications out of scattered archives and onto the Internet is creating opportunities for rediscovery, encounters with mostly forgotten works that have rarely been reprinted. Online search methods have made it easier to study the publication history of long-neglected works from this period, which in turn can facilitate the creation of new collections of local, regional, and national writing. As soon as we discovered interesting poems that appeared in local magazines, we used lines of verse enclosed within disambiguating quotation marks to identify ones most likely to have been written and first published in Boston. For example, a search for "I hear America singing" conducted on January 22, 2014, produced 98,600 hits, many for sites that contain Whitman's famous poem, while a search for the first line of many of the poems included here will produce a few, one, or no hits. For the most part, we attempted to exclude poems first published either abroad or in other American cities, though some non-Bostonian poems must surely have made it past our screening methods. For example, as not all texts published during the early national period have made it onto the Internet, some of the poems we identified as local may prove, when other early texts go online, to have been published first elsewhere. Still, even poems republished in the local magazines we searched can tell us something about the editors who decided to reprint them and the people who read their magazines. Interestingly, some of these "copied" poems were altered by Bostonian editors who felt free to print only parts of the original texts, change the titles, and tweak at will. Such editing can affect the meaning and impact of poems in ways that are worthy of detailed, comparative study. See the discussion of "EXTRACTS FROM FAWCETT'S CONTRAST" in the introduction to the "Politics" section and of "*A MOTHER's LOVE*" in the introduction to the "Family" section for striking examples of the way some reprinted poems differed radically from their sources. In the end, we decided to include a few imported poems that were not revised either because they inspired a response poem by a local writer or because they struck us as unusual and, therefore, indicative of what could be (re)printed and thought about in Boston at the time.

The sheer volume of verse being written in England during these decades meant that Boston editors could find and copy the pieces they thought would most delight and/or instruct readers. Still, the hundreds of poems written in Boston have a particular resonance for anyone interested in local history. Though many of even these poems can seem stilted and self-consciously poetic, the ones chosen for inclusion here struck us as remarkably fresh. Like folk art, indeed as folk-art poems, they can make up in directness, clarity, and charm what they sometimes lack in subtlety, polish, and formal variety. We chose poems that called out to us by providing access to the shops, streets, taverns, schools, and homes of Old Boston. By introducing us to a range of voices, personalities, and experiences, they can expand and deepen our sense of what was thought, felt, and written in those years.

While all of these poems provide glimpses into Old Boston, we actively sought out ones set at or related to particular locations. Poems whose speakers are grappling with life in the new city—either in the process of moving here or of moving away—proved irresistible. To twenty-first-century readers, the idea that a town of roughly twenty-three thousand people could have seemed daunting to the young man who describes his move here from the country in "THE STAGE COACH. INSCRIBED TO *MIRA*," which appeared in the October 1796 issue of the *Massachusetts Magazine*, is striking. And yet, before settling in to stay, the speaker is stunned by the clamor and bustle, the "horrid din . . . of coaches, hand-carts, trucks, and chaises." Entirely different views of the city and its port are conjured in "AN INTENDED INSCRIPTION, WRITTEN FOR THE MONUMENT ON BEACON-HILL, IN BOSTON, AND ADDRESSED TO THE PASSENGER" (*New England Quarterly Magazine*, April–June 1802), which celebrates the beauty of the capital, asking "Where stretch'd your sail, beneath what foreign sky / Did lov'lier landscapes ever charm your eye?" Works in this and other sections invite us to visit Court Street, ride horseback over Boston Neck, stop at a tavern on King Street, drop by a bookshop on State Street, chat with a young boy fishing in the Charles River, or buy a lottery ticket at the Exchange Building on Congress Street.

To illustrate the cultural resonance of the works included here, consider this brief, anonymously published poem about pigs that ran in the April 16, 1819, issue of the *New-England Galaxy and Masonic Magazine*. While no one would compare this poem to either a "summer's day" or a Shakespeare sonnet, its points of reference are fascinating:

BOSTON HOGS

Much has been said of Yankee pork;
And much of hogs in fam'd New York,
Where they the passengers will greet,
In their rough way, in every street.

But Boston folk's have better *notions*,
Restrain the swinish herd's commotions,

Keep them confin'd, and feed them well,
Then kill them off, to eat or sell.

Thus New York swine are lank and lean;
Bostonian, sleek, and fat and clean;
And those, just killed by Patterson,
Exceed New Yorkers three to one.

One would have to be pig-headed *not* to be drawn back in time by this amusing piece. Broad questions about when the Boston–New York rivalry began and specific ones about the identity of this mysterious Patterson leap off the page. According to an article that appeared in the *American Farmer* on May 7, 1819, Enoch Patterson was an "inn-keeper in Elm Street" who raised ten pigs to an average weight of 376 pounds. "They were viewed by numerous spectators when alive, who not only expressed their surprise at the extreme fatness, and fine form; but at the cleanliness and economy with which they were reared." Good to know. Beyond this, the poem offers a glimpse of the still-mixed landscape of downtown Boston eleven years before the cows that had grazed on the Common since the 1630s were permanently removed. And, of course, this is a provocative poem built around a series of delightfully taunting and invidious comparisons. Take *that* New York! Yo' mama grows skinny pigs and lets them run wild!

Coincidentally also about pigs, a poem called "A TRUE STORY" that ran in the February 19, 1820, issue of the *Ladies' Port Folio* may well be the first literary treatment of three enduring Boston themes: baked beans, traffic jams, and bad drivers. Check it out:

A TRUE STORY

It chanc'd one day, as people say,
    I think, in Charlestown* square,
A stage did wait to take some freight;
    Which often happens there.

A man did strive between to drive
    The stageman and the road;
But stage coach stood, like pile of wood,
    Still waiting for its load.

Now "Beverly,"* the man could see,
  All painted on the stage —
"You lazy sot, move that *bean-pot*,"
  He bellows, in a rage.

Stageman, in turn, replies with scorn,
  "Teamster, I'd let you work
Your forward way, but I must stay,
  Till I take in the *pork*."

*Charlestown: a town famous for the best of pork;
Beverly: a town famous for raising beans [original notes]

Like "BOSTON HOGS," "A TRUE STORY" draws us back to a time when coaches moved through and occasionally blocked the streets of a city still home to gardens and domesticated animals. Looking backward, it's hard not to recognize these drivers and hear their angry words echo through the centuries, while the focus on pork and beans (highlighted by notes in the original publication) evokes a dish that gave Boston its most enduring nickname.

Interactive gestures in the early magazines we reviewed — direct communication between the publishers and readers, editors and readers, editors and poets, poets and other poets, and poets and readers that appear in and around the poems — contribute to a sense of informality and community. In the first issue of the *Weekly Monitor*, a short-lived, nonsectarian, religious magazine published on Congress Street in 1817, the editors (Farnham and Badger) use both a prose note and a poem called "TO THE PATRONS OF THE WEEKLY MONITOR" to introduce their new publication. The note discusses practical matters, including the length and cost of the *Monitor*, noting that it would be both short and affordable. The poem is more personal, warmer in its appeal to readers, addressing "Friends to Religion — friends of Virtue, dear," and using a refrain that begins "To him . . . ," the ellipses being variously completed, as in, "To him who wanders from the path of life" or "To him who sinks by num'rous woes opprest." A final embrace concludes the poem: "Suffice to say — Although our work is small, / The Monitor shall be the *friend* of ALL." More playfully but in the same mode of direct address, the publisher of the *Thistle*, a magazine that lasted for just four weeks during the summer of 1807, set out this way in the first issue:

AN ORIGINAL WORK,
CONTAINING A GREAT MANY GOOD THINGS
By RODERIC ROVER, ESQ.
Published principally for the benefit of the purchasers, who will apply, if they have their wits about them, to the Bookstore of
ETHERIDGE & BLISS,
No. 12, Corn-Hill—Boston:
Where they will be indulged with a generous supply *for their money* . . . N.B. The Booksellers have agreed to remunerate *Roderic Rover*, and his brother *Joe*, [n.b. JOE is one syllable,] and all the rest of the family (one of the brightest families in the Commonwealth, between you and me), with enough to provide them raiment, and eatables and drink-ables, so long, as in their great kindness, they shall continue to honor the town with treats of original dainties.

Editors could reach out to readers, soliciting contributions of original work or comments on work in the magazine. In this way, Noah Worces-ter and Henry Ware Jr., the editors of the *Christian Disciple*, appended this note to a New Year's poem in their January 2, 1814, issue: "If the person, for whom it was particularly designed, or any other reader, shall be dissat-isfied with the sentiments expressed, and will forward a well written and candid reply, he may expect that it will find a place in our columns. Ed."

Distinguishing between a private cover letter and the work it describes is a convention of publication that had not yet become the norm. For in-stance, the headnote to the poem by Judith Sargent Murray that ran in the November 20, 1802, issue of the *Boston Weekly Magazine* served as com-munication between her and her editors:

MESSERS. EDITORS,
AS you have inserted my Cradle Piece so handsomely, I follow it by a BIRTH-DAY INVITATION, *written some months after, which if you give with equal accuracy, you shall hear again from a sincere well wisher to your very laudable undertaking.*

While this headnote conveys Murray's desire that her text be respected, the poem itself invites readers into the circle of her family by imagining what her infant daughter would, if she could speak, say to her one-year-older cousin. The anonymous poet whose "November Ramble" appeared in the December 1, 1806, issue of *Polyanthos* would not have been sur-prised to find the note he penned to the editor placed above the poem when it appeared:

> To the *EDITOR* of the *POLYANTHOS*.
> *SIR, I offer you the following Poem with diffidence. As to subject it has neither beginning, middle, nor end, and its verse is rough, unpolished and unmusical; but should its sentiments or descriptions meet your approbation, and in any degree counterbalance these defects, you will greatly favour me by inserting it in the Polyanthos. Yours, &c.*

Similarly, a note addressed to the editors of the *Boston Weekly Magazine* by the writer who published under the pen name "The Poetical Moralist" appears above a poem in the November 9, 1816, issue and provides both a conversational preface and a local setting:

> MESSERS EDITORS, During the pleasant weather of last summer, the orphans of the Female Asylum were several times conducted to the Common to walk, and enjoy, unconfined, the salubrity of the air. I had once the pleasure of meeting them there, and was a little impressed with the interesting scene; which suggested the following ideas.

The anonymous author of "LINES On reading a piece in the last Magazine, beginning, '*Hush, hush, thine heart, breathe not a sigh,*'" published in the *Boston Weekly Magazine* on November 22, 1817, felt impelled to respond directly to the author of a poem about finding consolation for grief. Explaining why he cannot take the "Hush, hush" poet's advice, the speaker of "LINES" regrets that the "minstrel's strain" cannot "erase / The gloom which clouds . . . [his] pallid cheek," and concludes by lamenting, "Oh, would to Heav'n my heart could join / In numbers soothing, soft, as thine." On a happier note, the author of "To the Editor *of the* Town *and* Country Magazine," which appeared in the final (January 1790) issue, celebrates the pleasure of reading books for the wise "precepts" they teach and the magazine for all of this:

> [W]hen I would know what the world is about,
> As who is took in, and who is turn'd out;
> How love and intrigue, how fashion and mode
> Among the *beau monde* are now understood;
> I turn a quick hand to your Magazine,
> And all in agreeable order is seen.

Provocative poems, especially on hot topics like the status of women, could elicit responses in verse. The reader who was outraged by a misogynist poem that the editors of the *Boston Weekly Magazine* copied in their

November 5, 1803, issue submitted his own poetic defense of abused wives, which ran a week later in the next (i.e., November 12) issue. "*Messrs* GILBERT & DEAN," he wrote in lines that the editors used as a headnote to the poem, "IF you think the enclosed lines worthy of a place, please publish them, as a contrast to the Epitaph on 'A Scolding Wife,' which appeared in your last Saturday's Magazine." The debate about gender that ran in the pages of a later version of the *Boston Weekly Magazine* in the late 1810s extended this practice of poem and anti-poem over several issues. Responding to misogynist poems by Ned Megrims (a pseudonym), the anonymous author of "TO NED MEGRIMS" — published in the February 7, 1818, issue — began, "THOU daring railer, vent'rest thou again / In demon's ink to dip thy sland'rous pen."

It was also standard practice for the editors of these magazines to respond in print to writers who submitted work, sometimes asking for revisions, more often announcing acceptances and rejections with terse expressions of praise or criticism. For example, in "ACKNOWLEDGMENTS TO CORRESPONDENTS" in the December 1791 issue of the *Massachusetts Magazine*, the editors applaud "Lines by Belinda" as "very acceptable" and note that "Maria's Elegy" is "worthy of her pen," but in the September 1793 issue of the same publication, the editors, in full rejection mode, tell the author of "Verses in memory of Mr. Paine" that "Poetry is not thy forte" and the author of "Stanzas on Hope" that "we also have a *hope* that such compositions may never put us in *fear* again." These editors were apparently willing to cross lines of good taste, as they did in responding in the September 1794 issue to a mourning poem submitted that summer: "We drop the tear of sympathy with *Celia* on the death of her friend; should we publish her elegy, we should occasion her, in the hour of dispassionate reflection additional sorrow." Ouch! Most strikingly, this snarky tone could appear even in the headnote to an accepted poem, as in this setup for "The Sacrifice," which ran in the March 27, 1816, issue of the *Recorder*: "[T]he following lines, the production of a lady of Massachusetts, though defective in rhyme, abound with legitimate poetry." Typical of this double messaging that sought both to solicit contributions and prescribe standards for them, the editors of the *Ladies' Port Folio* in their first issue in January 1820 addressed the following cautionary invitation to their readers:

> Our poetical correspondents are solicited to continue their favors. L. Y. R.'s article has been received, and shall have due consideration. While at the same time, we cannot but remark to those whom it may

concern, that punctuation, and grammatical accuracy, are by no means unimportant.

Lacking a sense of professional detachment or distance from unknown or known readers, poets frequently addressed themselves to the public in general or to specific people. Challenging, even taunting, readers, the partisan enigma that appeared in the October 31, 1817, issue of the *New England Galaxy and Masonic Magazine* demands, "Come tell me, if it is not past thy reach—/ Why is a beggar like George Canning's Speech?" More intimately, "Sephoronia" addresses "VERSES ON A SLEEPING DAUGHTER" (*Massachusetts Magazine*, January 1, 1793) to her "much lov'd infant," while "LINES, *Written by an old Planter, in the country, to his daughter*" (*Columbian Phenix and Boston Review*, March 1800), begins

> HOW, PHEBE, can I else but snarl,
> When you, who went a country girl,
> In habit frugal, neat and plain,
> That might attract some rural swain . . .

While it would be naive to assume that the first-person speakers in poems like this are the poets themselves, the immediacy of the dramatic framing draws on this perhaps fictive sense of direct address.

Statements about the poets' relations to their own work can also be found, as in the couplets that appeared in the July 26, 1796, issue of the *Nightingale*:

> CURST be the Verse, how well so e'er it flow,
> That tends to make one worthy man my foe;
> Give Virtue scandal—Innocence a fear;
> Or from the soft-eyed virgin steal a tear.

These lively, open, and engaged forms of communication were local variations on established practices of British magazine culture going back to the middle of the eighteenth century. Though far from unique, as practiced by editors and writers here, they nonetheless draw us into the small circle of Boston's literary culture during decades in which the population rose from about eighteen thousand in 1790 to about forty-three thousand in 1820.

Many of the poems here seem fresh for another reason as well: readers today are unlikely to have read them or know about their authors. By way of contrast, the names of American poets of the next generation—Henry Wadsworth Longfellow (1807–82), Edgar Allan Poe (1809–49), Walt Whitman (1819–92), and Emily Dickinson (1830–86), for instance—conjure something between a personality and a brand: Longfellow pious, Poe haunted, Dickinson reclusive, Whitman erotic. While each of these extremely limited descriptors only begins to capture the depth and range of these poets' work, each to some extent conditions our response by affecting what we expect. A consequence of the pre-professional, largely uncompensated context in which poets of the early national period worked is their anonymity: most published either without author attribution or with a one-word or one-letter pseudonym. And even the few who were known, at least by friends, are not widely remembered today. They include Robert Treat Paine (1731–1814), Judith Sargent Murray (1751–1820), Sarah Wentworth Morton (1759–1846), Susanna Haswell Rowson (1762–1824), David Hitchcock, and, toward the end of the period covered here, Lydia Huntley Sigourney (1791–1865), and Charles Sprague (1791–1875). Now largely forgotten by readers even in Boston, poems by these writers and their many anonymous contemporaries provide snapshots of the place where and the time when they were written and published.

Following the period covered by this collection, the rise of Romanticism with its emphasis on the artist as alienated outsider and/or visionary sage weakened the connection between poets and the particular places in which they lived and wrote. Poets in the early national period may have wanted to be recognized and compensated for their work, but they had to settle for something different: participating in conversations with other literate citizens. While many poets in these years deployed flowery language, invoked the muses, and struck poetic poses, others seized the opportunity to mock such gestures. For example, in "THE POET," a satirical piece that appeared in the *Ladies Afternoon Visitor* in 1807, "Zeuxis" makes fun of poets who think they ride on clouds and converse with Philomel. Like the rest of humanity, he insists, they catch colds, "blush, . . . mumble," and drink too much. He concludes,

> And though they live in air built houses,
> Their bodies are the home of louses;
> And thus like other men I shew it,
> Is that denominated Poet.

In 1832—by which time writers like Sprague, Nathaniel Parker Willis (1806–67), and Longfellow were starting to carve out professional identities and careers—a reviewer writing in the *New-England Magazine* highlighted this shift in how poets had come to be perceived:

> The common notion is, that a little madness is an essential ingredient in his composition; he is thought to move in a strangely eccentric orbit; in his words, actions, and opinions, he is supposed to obey laws and impulses peculiar to himself, and to be exempted, by the indulgence of mankind, from the responsibility which belongs to all others.

The poets whose mostly forgotten works are presented here were certainly capable of striking familiar poses (as lovers, drinkers, moralists, patriots, parents, mourners, even as poets), but they rarely seem to be participating in acts of self-branding or self-imitation. As a result, we are free to experience each poem on its own terms as a reflection of one more or less forgotten writer's engagement with whatever seemed worth noting at the time.

What we shouldn't expect is much in the way of formal variety. Poets of the following generation cultivated a sense of the relation between subject and form, fitting the latter to the former. Think of Longfellow's use of unrhymed, expansive hexameters in *Evangeline* (1847) or Poe's hypnotic use of internal and repetitive rhyme in "The Raven" (1845). Poe's account of how he composed his most famous poem captures both his professionalism and desire for originality:

> the feet employed throughout (trochees) consist of a long syllable followed by a short: the first line of the stanza consists of eight of these feet—the second of seven and a half (in effect two-thirds)—the third of eight—the fourth of seven and a half—the fifth the same—the sixth three and a half. Now, each of these lines, taken individually, has been employed before, and what originality the "Raven" has, is in their *combination into stanza*; nothing even remotely approaching this combination has ever been attempted. The effect of this originality of combination is aided by other unusual, . . . arising from an extension of the application of the principles of rhyme and alliteration.

With a few exceptions—including the jogging tetrameter in "THE STAGE COACH. INSCRIBED TO *MIRA*" and the blank verse of "Here comes Miss LIGHTHEAD" and William Cullen Bryant's (1794–1878) "Thanatopsis"—Boston's citizen poets defaulted into rhymed, tetrameter or pentameter couplets or quatrains regardless of the subject. Although the result was less artful verse, the directness of this method calls attention to the content and rhetoric of the poems: what the poets have to say and to whom they are saying it. Rather than remaining on the page and inviting formal analysis, many of their works jump out at and talk directly to imagined readers. Recovering their poems now allows us to eavesdrop on the conversations they contain.

❖ ❖ ❖

The Citizen Poets of Boston is divided into eight chronologically organized, subject-based sections that place differing voices and the experiences they convey into dialogue or debate. The anthology begins with a group of poems about the city of Boston itself. The young man who arrives in the 1796 "STAGE COACH" moves through his dark night of the soul, as

> Fell hypo [sadness] seiz'd me; in that hour
> I curst ambition's mighty power,
> Which led me from each former scene,
> The poplar grove, the level green,
> The rural sports from danger free,
> And happy hours, I past with thee.

Leaving the "heaven-befriended town" of Auburn behind, the speaker captures what must have been widely shared anxieties about the transition to the less natural, safe, and pleasant life of the city. Still, after a good night's sleep, he mingles "with the bustling city" and resolves to find his fate and fortune there. Not so the other young man, Sam, the speaker in "A LETTER TO TOM, IN THE COUNTRY" (*Boston Weekly Magazine*, December 7, 1816). Having moved to Boston to set up as a clothing merchant on his father's advice, Sam is perplexed "by a thousand ills." Disgusted with a city in which folly, greed, and fashion rule, he despairs about his chance of growing wealthy or finding a wife, and makes up his mind "to leave this place" and return to the country:

> Alas! Dear Tom, I curse the day,
> That put me in this irksome way;
> That led me on in hope of gain,
> From paths of ease to paths of pain.

The poems in this volume about men and women also draw us back through time and space. Cultural debates come to life in this section, as the proper roles for both genders are at stake throughout. In "SONG.

I courted a girl that I long wished to marry," included in the *Scourge* on August 28, 1811, a cynical young man who has difficulty interesting the woman he's attracted to buys a lottery ticket that enriches him to the extent that his future wife finds him acceptable. In other works, laments about abusive wives are juxtaposed with assertively feminist voices, while the rights of women are broadly imagined by some poets and limited to the domestic sphere by others. Readers may well be surprised by female speakers who declare their right either to choose their own husbands or "to [live and] die an old maid." Along with traditional love poems, warnings about excessive passion, laments about quarreling in marriage, and celebrations of female modesty, expect to encounter women who want to "wear the breeches."

In the poems that deal directly with politics some writers embrace patriotic themes like the celebration of George Washington (1732–99) while others promote universal benevolence or plead for mistreated subgroups. Among these, some poems gain power through the grounding of opinions in vivid imagery. They take us to the prison cells of Marie Antoinette (1755–93) and of an unnamed but too harshly judged murderer. They contrast innocent street sweepers with self-serving brokers, doctors, and lawyers. A poem by the English minister-poet Joseph Fawcett (c.1758–1804) included in this section was extracted from a longer version he included in the 1798 volume of his poems. Chosen for republication by the editors of the antiwar *Christian Disciple*, it articulates a startlingly radical, pre-Marxist and pacifist politics that one might not expect to find so early (1816) in an American magazine. In this way, Fawcett's work as extracted provides an introduction to the rising peace movement in Boston that followed the end of both the War of 1812 and the Napoleonic Wars. Overall, the international reach of many of the works in this section reminds us that Bostonians—while engaged in local, regional, and national debates —looked both east and south across the ocean as citizens of an evolving trans-Atlantic world.

Poems about the family reveal the dynamism of domestic life in these years. In Judith Sargent Murray's 1790 denunciation of corporal punishment for "trembling youth," a new emphasis on affection between parents and children shines forth. In Susanna Haswell Rowson's celebration of Thanksgiving, gratitude to God is subsumed in a poem that celebrates warmth, light, food, and wit enjoyed in an atmosphere of "sportive love and sacred friendship."

Some of the poems that focus on work and the professions are animated by timeless concerns about the honesty of lawyers, the effectiveness of doctors, and the hypocrisy or intolerance of preachers. But others are more specific to their time and place, introducing us to mechanics, clerks, teachers, students, and poets.

Signs of an evolving debate can be found in the poems on pleasure and the good life. "BACCHUS's SHRINE" (*Massachusetts Magazine*, 1796) makes the case for the benefits of drinking and mocks grave, proud, and sour men who subsist on water and, as a result, succumb to "grief and mad despair." Also in this section, joyful celebrations of the sheer pleasures of kissing and drinking appear along with poems like "PARODY" (*Boston Weekly Magazine*, 1804), which follows a young hedonist who drops out of school and ends up in prison where he is forced to "wear clanking chains" and "wishes oft to die."

A group of playful poems collected near the end of the anthology—including riddles, rebuses, anagrams, and acrostics—challenged their first readers to solve puzzles based on information available when the poems were published. For this reason, they may shift you into Internet search mode. Puzzle poems that went unsolved at the time—such as R. S. G.'s rebus (*Boston Weekly Magazine*, November 12, 1803)—are particularly enticing and challenging. Insofar as solving these orphaned rebuses requires a familiarity with life in Boston two centuries ago, they call us back in time in search of clues based on culturally specific contexts.

The final section gathers poems about death—including epitaphs, tributes, meditations, and drollery—written either about a person who has died or the nature of mortality. The visits to graveyards provided by these poems are appropriate enough for a collection that begins with a young man setting out in life. And the range of situations described—including the grieving of a forlorn mother; the declaration of faith in a forthcoming, better life; and the lamentation of a man whose mother died when he was born—suggests that thinking about death and dying was in those times as varied as considerations of any other part of life.

As you make your way through this collection, you will undoubtedly notice that many of the poems could fit in more than one section. Specific poems in the section on men and women, for example, resonate with other poems on the family, pleasure, work, politics, play, and death. For instance, "STANZAS TO MARIA ANTONIETTA" in the "Politics" section sees its eponymous character as a woman facing execution bereft of family and friends, while poems in the section on death that deal with the loss of a parent or child add to the sense we have of family life at this time. One way we gained insight into these works was by considering which section to put them in. So, if you question where some of them appear, you will, in effect, be pulling a chair up to our editing roundtable.

This project has been both a treasure hunt and a feast. By conjuring places and people long gone — allowing readers to share the passions and convictions, experiences and ideas of another time — the poems collected here are engaging, even intoxicating. So be forewarned: Time travel is inherently perilous. Once you board the stagecoach back to Old Boston, you may find that the places you visit and the people you encounter draw you in. You may well never want to leave that tavern, push back from that Thanksgiving table, walk away from the bedside of that sleeping daughter, or leave the grave of that much-loved child.

If you find yourself entranced, there are ways to continue exploring the publications from which the works here were extracted. Online access to all of the magazines included here is available through the American Periodical Series database, and many of them can be found through open-access Google Book searches. Even better, searches in the online catalogs of the Boston Public Library and Massachusetts Historical Society and in the Worldcat database will lead you to local sites where you will be able to sit and read through whole issues and annual volumes of these rare, old publications. The thrill of connecting to long-forgotten writing, hearing the voices of Bostonians who helped shape American culture in the first decades of our national life and whose works bring the past into sharp relief awaits you in the Rare Books Room of the Boston Public Library in Copley Square, at the Massachusetts Historical Society a mile west on Boylston Street, and in other area archives and collections, both private and public. Following these leads, you will be able to find poems in this volume in their original form — with antiquated lettering, line spacing, and punctuation. And you'll be able to read other poems and discover the stories and essays that often appeared side by side with them. Access to these works has never been easier, as you'll see. The hard part may be returning to a world in which Boston long ago lost not only its neck but its shared sense of intimacy as well.

NOTES

1. Frank Luther Mott, *A History of American Magazines, 1741–1850* (Cambridge, MA: Belknap Press of Harvard University Press, 1957), 200.

2. On the international distribution and cross-influence of poetry, see *The Traffic in Poems: Nineteenth-Century Poetry and Transatlantic Exchange*, Meredith L. McGill, ed. (New Brunswick, NJ: Rutgers University Press, 2008). On the ideal of citizenship grounded not only in political activity but also in the production and consumption

of literature during the early national period, see Michael T. Gilmore, "The Literature of the Revolutionary and Early National Periods," in *The Cambridge History of American Literature*, vol. 1: 1590–1820 (Cambridge, MA: Cambridge University Press, 1994; 2008), 539–694; Michael Warner, *The Letters of the Republic: Publication and the Public Sphere in Eighteenth-Century America* (Cambridge, MA: Harvard University Press, 1990); and Catherine O'Donnell Kaplan, *Men of Letters in the Early Republic* (Chapel Hill, NC: University of North Carolina Press, 2008).

3. Lyon N. Richardson, *A History of Early American Magazines* (New York: Thomas Nelson and Sons, 1931), 360; Mott, *History of American Magazines*, 176; Neal A. Edgar, *History and Bibliography of American Magazines, 1810–1820* (Metuchen, NJ: Scarecrow Press, 1975), 33–34; Edward E. Chielens, *American Literary Magazines: The Eighteenth and Nineteenth Centuries* (New York: Greenwood Press, 1986), 245; Jared Gardner, *The Rise and Fall of Early American Magazine Culture* (Chicago: University of Illinois Press, 2012); David S. Shields, ed., *American Poetry: The Seventeenth and Eighteenth Centuries* (New York: Library of America, 2007).

COMING TO BOSTON

Unknown artist, stagecoach of 1800
Courtesy of the Bostonian Society

In 1789 when the *Massachusetts Magazine* began publishing on what was then called Newbury Street, Boston was both old and new. Its first English colonizers, led by Governor John Winthrop (1588–1649), built their "city upon a hill" in the middle of the seventeenth century and in the process developed a print culture unrivaled in the Americas. The American Revolution began in Boston, and events here—including the Boston Massacre, Tea Party, siege of the city, and battles of Concord, Lexington, and Bunker Hill—drew on earlier acts of colonial resistance that set the tone for what would follow. During the decades after the Revolution, Bostonians debated new ideas about men, women, parents, children, workers, professions, nature, literature, politics, history, and culture broadly defined. In some of this writing, Boston itself figured as a primary subject in a number of interesting ways.

The poems collected in this section represent the diverse deployment of the city as both a geographical setting and a place where specific values prevailed, for better or worse. To the young, anonymous speaker of "THE STAGE COACH. INSCRIBED TO *MIRA*" (1796), which simulates the clumping rhythm of a horse-drawn journey, Boston looms as an urban alternative to his old life in the country. Both the potentially invidious nature of the rural-urban contrast and the awkwardness of his big move are made clear in the opening lines in which he promises to sing about

> How erst [first] I rural bliss resign'd
> Left Mira, and my heart behind,
> And how, like fortune's foot ball toss'd on
> I quick was tumbled into Boston.

Depressed on arrival, the speaker is shocked to find himself in a world of "smoke, . . . toil, and care." Happily, like many young people who would move into cities in the nineteenth century, he soon cheers up and resolves to mingle "with the bustling city" as he begins life anew. Like several of the poems in this section, "THE STAGE COACH" vividly captures the landscape, interior and exterior, through which its speaker moves—as in this description of a meal he eats with other passengers at a roadside inn:

> Behold us round the festive board,
> With tough beef steak and butter stor'd
> See ruddy Ruth bring in her toast;
> See cider pitcher, brought by host;
> While hostess round with coffee serves,

Too weak by far to hurt the nerves;
While many a merry jest goes round,
And bursting laughter shakes the ground.

To the author of the "Epigram: As two Divines" (*Massachusetts Magazine*, October 1796), Boston is the perfect place to set a poem that ridicules religious intolerance, while for the author of "ON THE LICENTIOUS-NESS OF THE MANNERS OF THE PRESENT DAY" (*Boston Weekly Magazine*, August 11, 1804), Boston is the perfect setting for a moralistic rant about the misbehavior of young men who forget the value of friendship and "pure love," indulging instead in "midnight orgies" in the "wanton arms" of "syrens"! James Allen's "AN INTENDED INSCRIPTION, WRITTEN FOR THE MONUMENT ON BEACON-HILL" (1802) castigates the British for having cut down the Liberty Tree during the Siege of Boston and celebrates the stump ("the dear remain") as the place where liberty "first rear'd" its "illumin'd fane." Similarly, while it takes a dim view of the event it describes, "LINES *on the Elm Tree, which for many years has been the ornament of Court-Street, and was cut down in the beginning of this month*" (*Monthly Anthology, and Boston Review*, April 1, 1805) also provides glimpses of the urban street life the vanquished tree had covered:

> The noisy artist's grating sound,
>   The lawyer's pedant phrase
> The merchant's cant shall cease around,
>   And list to rural lays.

Seen as an act of cruelty and avarice that displaced nesting birds and undermined "rural virtues," the destruction of the tree initiates a debate about urban development that still seems familiar.

"ANACREON IMITATED" and "FRAGMENT. As I walk'd on the banks of Charles' briny flood" take us to specific Bostonian locations and introduce us to quite different people. In "ANACREON," we meet a sturdy, middle-class fellow staying at "Whitcomb's or Exchange hotel" who enjoys the pleasures of this world—including food, wine, and family—and doesn't think or care much about life after death. In "FRAGMENT," the speaker moralizes following his encounter with a young boy who is fishing without a hook, noting that many adults foolishly waste their time too:

> I've seen fellow mortals on follies await,
>   And angle for pleasure and joy;

They've toil'd all their days, both early and late,
Alas! like a novice without hook or bait,
And succeeded like this little boy.

Like "THE STAGE COACH," three other poems in this section—"A
LETTER TO TOM, IN THE COUNTRY," "Dear Jack, I am no more the
clown," and "JONATHAN'S JOURNEY TO BOSTON"—allow us to fol-
low young men who travel to Boston and either stay or retreat. In "A LET-
TER TO TOM" (*Boston Weekly Magazine*, December 7, 1816), which might
have been written by the same "Sam" who wrote about the fishing boy, the
speaker apologizes for not writing sooner and goes on to explain why he
will soon move back to the country and farm life. Persuaded by his father
to move to Boston and open a clothing shop, Sam is unable to make a go
of it. Thwarted by usurious moneylenders and rapacious landlords, and
frustrated by "shoppers" who rarely buy anything, he finds it impossible
to thrive. Here and there in this collection, poets who wrote two hundred
years ago express unsurprisingly antiquated opinions, as the anonymous
author of "A LETTER TO TOM" does in offering this bigoted characteri-
zation of the men who thwarted his hopes:

'Tis not that here's *no trade* at all,
Nor that my *profits*, Tom, are small,
That I complain—no, surely no—
But 'tis, that *half* we make must go
To *Jews*, whose *hearts* are not content,
But when they *shave* at *three per cent*!
That *landlords*, who of wealth possess'd,
Should for their *rents* take all the rest!
Not even leave one cent for those
Who furnish us so *cheap* with clothes.

Since we have no desire to conceal such culturally specific and, perhaps,
widely shared views even when they offend modern sensibilities, we in-
clude poems as they ran, assuming that our readers will make allowances
for the centuries-long evolution of thinking. It's worth noting that the an-
tisemitic stereotype in "A LETTER TO TOM" is part of a broader, satirical
critique of the urban populace:

Ah! surely, Tom, *Dad* was deceiv'd,
And oft I've set me down, and griev'd

That man should be by *follies* rul'd,
And woman still in *fashions* school'd.
What he had seen was a mere hoax—
A *notion* of the Boston folks.
'Tis true they all a shopping go,
But yet 'tis only for a show—
Although from shop to shop they fly,
Believe me, Tom, they seldom buy!

Striking a lighter but still satirical tone, "Dear Jack I am no more the clown" (*Boston Weekly Magazine*, February 20, 1918) mocks the fashion-consciousness rife in a Boston populated by "beau," "fops," and "dandies" who dress like monkeys and "lounge around dry good shops." Refusing to wear "lady's stays" (i.e., corsets) because "they'd squeeze / [his] marrow bones to jelly nice, / And stop [his] windpipe in a trice," the speaker concludes by describing an evening at the theater during which he amusingly fails to understand what he is seeing. The penultimate poem in this section, "JONATHAN'S JOURNEY TO BOSTON" (*Ladies' Port Folio*, March 25, 1820) offers another character who fails to comprehend the world he visits and then decides to leave. Crossing over Boston Neck a half hour before sunset, Jonathan is jostled by crowds in the streets and exhausted from his trip. Marveling at the height of buildings, he searches for an inn and settles on one that costs more than he had hoped to pay. The rest of the poem describes his response to two fires, neither of which he understands. To warm up at the inn, he stands with his back to a new-fangled, peat-burning fireplace, blocking other guests from the heat and burning his own pants "to a crisp." When he goes out for a walk, he falls in with people rushing toward a fire, puzzles over the use of water pumps to put it out, gets lost finding his inn, and in a state of numb confusion, resolves to go home:

Such being the noise, and confusion in town,
Near father and mother I'll fix myself down,
Take care of the farm—wed *fair* Molly Brown—
And live till I die, a plain good-hearted clown.

Down from Vermont, this Jonathan is clearly based on the already popular New England bumpkin figure who had a long career even before Royall Tyler (1757–1826) made use of him in *The Contrast* (1787). But it's worth noting that, however conventional his ignorance and naivety were at the time this poem was published, this Jonathan's adventure in the big city provides access to specific features of urban life, including the possibility of getting lost and encounters with sophisticated city folk and advanced technologies.

Kristin L. Canfield, a member of our research team, has noted the intermingling of local and trans-Atlantic motifs in the final poem in this section, "In Boston." Published in the *Universalist Magazine* on June 10, 1820, it recounts an argument that took place in 1814 between interlocutors identified only as "A" and "B." When "A" failed to refute the truth of Universalism, presumably the notion that all people are redeemed and heaven-bound, he argued that it would be dangerous to "proclaim" this truth, presumably because doing so would undermine public morality. "B's" response came soon after and was based on good news from Europe that the treaty of Ghent, which ended the War of 1812, had been signed. Amid universal jubilation, "B" ironically said, "But tell it not 'twill harm some one I fear." The interweaving of local, national, and international beliefs and events in so few lines reminds us that the port city of Boston was then as it is now open to the world.

THE STAGE COACH.
INSCRIBED TO *MIRA*.

How erst[†] I rural bliss resign'd
Left Mira, and my heart behind,
And how, like fortune's foot ball, toss'd on,
I quick was tumbled into Boston,
I sing, dear maid, in doggrel rhyme
And numbers, as the theme, sublime;
For whether I'm a dunce or poet,
I feel above prose, or below it.
  'Twas now that hour, when darkness deep
Buried the world in silent sleep,
Supine I lay, and blissful dreams
Had finish'd all my hopes and schemes,
In Auburn's heaven-befriended town
Peaceful for life had fix'd me down;
Indulgent heaven had kindly lent
A competency and content;
Just had I sworn my life should be
Sacred to friendship, love, and thee —
That is to say, 'twas three o'clock,
When at my chamber door a knock,
That mock'd a clap of rattling thunder,
Burst Morpheus'[†] grateful bands asunder,
And with the rapid lightning's rage,
Hurl'd me, half craz'd, into the stage.
There, squeez'd amid a silent throng,
Of rich, and poor, and old, and young,
We soon drove off that peaceful plain,
Where Mira and the virtues reign.
  Now we move thro forest drear,
Not a sound salutes the ear,
Save the rumbling carriage wheel,
Save the plaintive whippoorwill,
Save the distant housedog's howl,
And the hooting of the owl.
Soon morn with
Smiling face came on,
Held forth her blazing torch, the sun,

Which lighted me to lay before ye,
Of passengers an inventory;
Namely, a dame, in weight a ton,
Another with an infant son,
A rural nymph, in homespun neat,
With these fill'd up the hindmost seat,
An antient maiden, prim and short,
A beau quack doctor, just the sort,
A jovial priest with lungs of Stentor[†]
And Mr. I filled up the center.
In politics a blustering diver[†]
Sat forward to dispute with driver.
    As day advanc'd, "our tongues were loos'd,"
And various chat our minds amus'd;
Till at a tavern, full of glee,
We sat, as Paul at sight of three.[†]
Behold us round the festive board,
With tough beef steak and butter stor'd;
See ruddy Ruth bring in her toast;
See cider pitcher, brought by host;
While hostess round with coffee serves,
Too weak by far to hurt the nerves;
While many a merry jest goes round,
And bursting laughter shakes the ground.
    Now the landlord's bill is paid,
Mount the stage, both man and maid,
Each set up a merry giggle,
Huddle in all higgle piggle.
Loud the driver smacks his whip,
And the frighted horses skip;
Swift the clattering carriage bounds,
Over rocks and rising grounds;
Pleasure beams in every eye,
Song and laughter reach the sky.
Not a moment's stay is made,
Save some budget to unlade,
Save for Bacchus to bewine us,
Fellow traveler leave or join us,
Or our tatter'd tackling tie,
Till a signpost meets the eye,

And the tavern's welcome dome
Bids us make ourselves at home.
　　Here our drink and talk are various,
Brandy strong, and punch nectareous,
Shatter'd stage, and coach and six,
Wit and war, and politics;
Till dinner our attention draws
To better work for hungry jaws.
Huge Indian pudding on vast platter,
Whose very sight makes Yankey's fatter;
Potatoes on the dish high pil'd
At which St. Patrick might have smil'd;
English roast beef, so stout, so fat,
Even Bache[†] would change to Aristocrat;
With cider in a copious flood,
Compos'd a treat so plain, so good,
Temperance and luxury might mate,
And feast together on one plate.
　　Thus dinner done, and light each heart,
Again in joyful mood we start,
Prepar'd with drink, of noise creative,
To astonish many a rural native.
But blazing Sol soon stopt our courses,
Melted our courage, and our horses,
And left us as he hasted down,
To creep, like cumbrous snails, to town.
　　As to their journey's end time brought 'em,
Companions dropp'd, "like leaves in autumn,"
And evening, clad in dismal black,
Found but the priest, myself and quack.
A solemn stillness round us hung;
Sunk was each heart, and mute each tongue;
Fell hypo seiz'd me; in that hour
I curst ambition's mighty power,
Which led me from each former scene,
The poplar grove, the level green,
The rural sports from danger free,
And happy hours, I past with thee.
Forward I look'd from views, so fair,
To city smoke, and toil, and care;

School-keeping saw, depress'd with scorn,
Saw prose, poor, ragged and forlorn,
Saw poetry's dread ills assail,
The garret mean and gloomy jail,
Till horrid din at once amazes,
Of coaches, handcarts, trucks, and chaises,
Awakes me from my reverie,
And from the carriage sets me free.
        Again refresh'd in noisy tavern,
I crawl to bed in tomblike cavern,
Where wearied travellers without number,
Enjoy the sweets of deathlike slumber,
And insects multiform appear,
Too shocking for a lady's ear.
Thus, while this seems death's gloomiest hive,
I am most "tremblingly alive,"
And, ere sweet sleep I close my eyes in,
I fall to serious moralizing,
Extract a line from Shakespear's page,
And swear that "All the world's a stage,"
And every passenger, who takes it,
Has both an entrance and an exit,
And each plays many antic tricks,
His different ages being six.
        Thro infancy first see him go,
A gloomy forest, pav'd with wo.
To childhood next he wanders on,
There's blest with reason's rising sun.
In youth thro frolic's maze he's wheeling,
Or to his mistress sighing, kneeling.
Blest with a wife at manhoods's noon,
He enjoys a rapturous honeymoon.
Then downward slides life's warming sun,
Decrepid age comes slowly on,
Relations, friends, acquaintance leave him,
And present, past, and future grieve him.
"Last scene of all," which quick must end him,
The parson and the quack attend him;
The fates his exit soon determine,
And down he lies, the food of vermin.

When morn arose with smiles so pretty,
I mingled with the bustling city,
Resolved, whatever be my fate,
Let the world love or let it hate,
Let me be batchellor or married,
Or in a coach or cart be carried,
Or rich, or poor, or grave, or mellow,
To live and die, a clever fellow.

Anonymous, *Massachusetts Magazine*, October 1796

†*erst*: first; *Morpheus*: god of dreams; *Stentor*: loud-voiced herald of the Greek forces during the Trojan War; *diver*: one who dives deeply into a subject; *Paul at sight of three*: Acts 9 tells the story of Paul the Apostle's conversion: blinded for three days, Paul (called Saul) miraculously recovers his sight, is baptized, and eats some food; *Bache*: Benjamin Franklin Bache (1769–98): grandson of Benjamin Franklin, a journalist, publisher, and advocate for Jeffersonian Republicanism.

————

Epigram [As two Divines, their ambling steeds bestriding]

As two Divines, their ambling steeds bestriding,
In merry mood o'er Boston neck were riding,
At length a simple structure met their sight,
From which the felon takes his hempen flight,
When, sailor like, he squares accounts with hope,
His all depending on a single rope;
"Ah where, my friend," cried one, "where now were *you*
Had yonder gallows been allowed its due?"
"*Where*," said the other in sarcastic tone,
"Why *where*—but riding into town *alone*."

Cam., *Massachusetts Magazine*, October 1796

————

AN INTENDED INSCRIPTION, WRITTEN FOR THE MONUMENT ON BEACON-HILL, IN BOSTON, AND ADDRESSED TO THE PASSENGER

Where stretch'd your sail, beneath what foreign sky
Did lov'lier landscapes ever charm your eye?
Could fancy's fairy pencil, Stranger! say,
E'en dipt in dreams, a nobler scene pourtray?

Behold yon vales, whose skirts elude your view,
And mountains fading to aerial blue!
Along their bow'ry shades how healthy toil
Alternate sports, or tends the mellow soil.
See rural towns mid groves and gardens rise,
And eastward—where the stretching ocean lies,
Lo! Our fair capital sublimes the scene,
New *Albion's* pride, and ocean's future queen;
How o'er the tradeful port august she smiles,
Her sea-like haven boasts an hundred isles,
Whence hardy commerce swells the lofty sails
O'er arctic seas, and mocks the polar gales,
Thence tides of wealth the wafting breezes bring,
And hence e'en culture feels its vital spring.

These scenes our Sires from rugged nature wrought,
Since—what dire wars their patriotic race have fought!
Witness yon tracts, where first the Briton bled,
Driv'n by our youth redoubted PERCY[†] fled:
There BREED[†] ascends, and BUNKER'S bleeding steeps,
Still o'er whose brow abortive Vict'ry weeps;
What Trophies since! The gaze of after times,
Rear'd *Freedom's* empire o'er our happy climes!

But hence, fond Stranger, take a nobler view,
See yon shorn elm,* whence all these glories grew.
Here, where the armed foe presumptuous trod,
Trampled our shrines, and even mouth'd our GOD,
His vengeful hand, deep as the parent-root,
Lopt each grown branch, and ev'ry suckling shoot;
Because beneath her consecrated shade
Our earliest vows to LIBERTY were paid.
High from *her ALTAR* blew the heaven-caught fire,
While all our wealth o'erhung the kindling pyre.
How at the deed the nations stood aghast,
As on the pile our plighted lives we cast!

O! if an alien from our fair domains,
The blood of *Britain*, hapless, taint your veins,
Pace o'er that hallow'd ground with awful tread,
And tears, atoning, o'er yon relick shed;
But if, American! Your lineage springs,
From Sires, who scorn the pedigree of kings,

A Georgian born you breathe the tepid air,
Or on the breezy banks of *Delaware*,
Or hardy *Hampshire* claim your haughty birth,
Revere yon root, and kiss its nurt'ring earth;
O be its fibres fed with flowing springs,
Whence rose our empires o'er the thrones of kings;
E'en now descend, adore the dear remain,
Where first rear'd Liberty's illumin'd fane,
There all the race, while times revolve shall come,
As pilgrims flock to MECCA's idol'd tomb.

James Allen, *New England Quarterly Magazine*, April–June, 1802.

elm: The stump of the Liberty Tree [original note].
†*Percy*: Hugh Percy, second duke of Northumberland (1742–1817); *Breed*: Breed's Hill
where much of the Battle of Bunker Hill took place.

————

ON THE LICENTIOUSNESS OF THE MANNERS OF THE PRESENT DAY.

To false delights the youth of *Boston* fly,
    Who court for happiness the wanton's arms;
Who dart on all the fond inflaming eye,
    And *choiceless*, yield to all for *gold* her charms.
When in the syren's fond embrace you sigh,
    And on her lip impress the burning kiss,
Doth *friendship* mingle with the unhallowed joy,
    Or *love's* pure spirit swell the page of bliss?
When droops enjoyment, what is then the fair?
    A *flower*, that blooms, but quickly doom'd to fade;
A *sun*, that pours a momentary glare,
    And, 'mid the tempest, sinks beneath the shade.
O swains! To modesty's fair daughters turn,
    By *mental* beauty let your hearts be led;
Bid, by your flight, the venal fair one mourn,
    And press in tears her solitary bed.
When round your neck her fondling arms she glues,
    And bent to please, exhausts each winning art;
With false delights she shamefully subdues,
    And leads the passions captive, not the *heart*.

Their midnight orgies whilst they madly hold,
    I, of a tender maid shall be possess'd;
What bliss her tender beauties to unfold,
    And sooth my slumbers on her faithful breast!
Time, from her bosom, all its snows may steal,
    His iron hand her cheek's pure blush invade;
Still to my A—— will I fondly kneel,
    And love her more, when all her roses fade.
Who spurns the weeping fair one from his breast,
    Hard is his heart—in every virtue poor;
Hard is his heart, to wound the fair distrest,
    Who sighs that she can charm his eye no more.
Cruel, to bid with grief her bosom heave,
    Because her cheeks no longer glowing warm;
Base, to forget the joys her beauty gave,
    And oh, forget it, *faded in his arms*!

A. Q., Boston Weekly Magazine, August 11, 1804

———

LINES *on the Elm Tree, which for many years has been the ornament of Court-Street, and was cut down in the beginning of this month.*

Yon mutilated trunk but late
    The fairest Elm tree rais'd,
That e'er adorn'd the rural state,
    Or e'er by bard was prais'd.

'Twas there I stood, when on my mind
    A voice exulting broke,
Which pierc'd its branch's stubborn rind,
    And thus triumphant spoke.

"Where art's ambitious reign presumes
    To curb mild nature's sway,
Above the towers and shining domes,
    My verdant honours play.

"With foes beleaguer'd still my race
    Holds footing in the land—
Lo, like a castle here I grace
    The city's midmost stand:

"Confiding in whose sheltering care,
    From distant grove and glade
Shall all the woodland spirits dare
    Its hostile streets invade.

"The feather'd race shall hither throng,
    Obedient to my call;
And pour in choirs the forest song
    From every echoing wall.

"The noisy artist's grating sound,
    The lawyer's pedant phrase,
The merchant's cant shall cease around,
    And list to rural lays.

"The prisoner from his grate shall view
    My green tops flourish fair,
And bless each bird upon the bough,
    Whose song beguiles his care.

"She, on the gently waving bough,
    Shall build the frequent nest,
And be at peace, while all below
    Unquiet sense molest.

"And as feign'd oracles of yore
    The delphick laurel shook,
And voices strange at midnight hour
    Have through my branches spoke,

"The pilgrim bard shall oft again
    Beneath my shadow stop;
And heard by him, the mystick strain
    Shall wake the cheering hope.

"While one green offspring of the grove
    Shall in this town abide,
Shall poetry and spotless love
    Find dwellings there beside;

"And as my glowing branches tower
    Above the structures proud,
One day restor'd to pristine power
    Shall he contemn the crowd."

Alas, how vain the high pretence!
    The blasted spot behold—
The boastful Elm lies scatter'd hence,
    Like murder'd beauty cold.

What demon spoke the fatal word
    That fell'd it to the ground?
No Tancred[†] with his heaven-lent sword
    Could give the impious wound.

'Twas av'rice—av'rice's cruel arm,
    Its fall lamented brought;
The love of wealth's more potent charm
    Than e'er Amida[†] wrought.

And therefore I will hate the man,
    His tasteless mind detest,
Who first conceiv'd the ruthless plan,
    Or wrought the deed unblest.

Ye rural virtues flee the town,
    Ye simple manners flee;
Your last stronghold was broken down
    When fell that beauteous tree.

Sure, nature heard the stern command
    To leave it on that day;
The ancient habits of the land
    To pride and art gave way.

For by this Elm's sad overthrow
   I'll fix the gloomy date,
When times shall hard and evil grow,
   And man lament his fate.

Anonymous, Monthly Anthology, and Boston Review, April 1, 1805

[†]*Tancred*: King of Sicily (1189–94), rumored to have been given the sword Excalibur by Richard I; *Amida*: Saint Acacius, bishop of Amida, Turkey, from 400 to 425 CE[?].

————

ANACREON[†] IMITATED
Ἐπὶ μυρσίναις τερείναις,[†] &c.

In that snug mansion, where I dwell,
At Whitcomb's or Exchange hotel,
On wholesome viands let me dine,
And stimulate with generous wine;
Swift as the rapid chariot's way,
We haste to mingle with our clay.
What can I care, when dead and gone,
For coffin gilt, or costly stone,
Standing at head and feet erect,
With prose and poetry bedeck'd?
Rather on me, while yet I live,
Bestow, if aught you wish to give,
Employment good, and handsome pay,
With which to pass my time away,
Children enrich with education,
And fit them for a decent station.
This while I've life—and when without it,
Bury–and make no fuss about it.

Anonymous, Monthly Anthology, and Boston Review, September 1, 1810

[†]*Anacreon*: Greek poet (582–485 BCE); *Ἐπὶ μυρσίναις τερείναις*: "upon [the] soft myrtles" (Greek), the opening line of Anacreon's thirty-second ode, which makes most of the points reproduced here, though without the middle-class aspirations and Boston setting.

FRAGMENT. [As I walk'd on the banks of Charles' briny flood]

As I walk'd on the banks of Charles' briny flood,
    A boy I descried very pensive,
Approach'd to the place where he busily stood,
To learn if from this would result any good,
    Conferring with youth inoffensive.

Respecting his age, I enquir'd, and his name,
    (For this I conceiv'd no intrusion)
And why thus alone, to the river he came,
Which known to his parents, they'd certainly blame—
    At which he seem'd wrapp'd in confusion.

"To catch little fishes, which play in the brook,"
    He reply'd, and looked up with a smile;
He reach'd me the rod, which from him I took,
When lo! there was neither a *bait* or a *hook*!
    But it served his young hours to beguile.

I immediately left him his time to employ,
    Which I knew would be check'd by my stay;
Well pleased that a moral might flow from a boy,
Whose whole occupation was prattle and toy,
    And pond'ring pursu'd my lone way.

Now reflecting on man, how many said I,
    At this moment are wasting their time,
Nor regard the choice hours which speedily fly,
While they in embraces of idleness lie,
    And exult in her charms so benign.

I've seen fellow mortals on follies await,
    And angle for pleasure and joy;
They've toil'd all their days, both early and late,
Alas! like a novice without hook or bait,
    And succeeded like this little boy.

Sam, *Boston Weekly Magazine*, November 16, 1816

A LETTER TO TOM, IN THE COUNTRY

MESSERS. EDITOR — I shall make no apology for sending this "Letter,"
but only say, as the Almanack Maker says of his work — *calculated* for the
Magazine, but will *serve* for any other place.

DEAR TOM, your letter came to hand,
And pleas'd I am to understand,
That you enjoy such perfect health;
A blessing, friend, more dear than wealth.
I must confess I have done wrong,
Thus to neglect my friend so long;
I promised oft to write, I know,
And should have done it long ago,
But things have turned out bad, I find —
A thousand ills perplex my mind:
That when I sit to take my pen,
I rise, and — lay it down again,
I wish I ne'er had left that spot,
Those pleasing sports, our rural cot,
Nor ventur'd here where folly's pow'r,
Destroys pure friendship's social hour.
Alas! dear Tom, I curse the day,
That put me in this irksome way;
That led me on in hope of gain,
From paths of ease to paths of pain.
But 'twas a father's plan, you see,
To make a *dashing chap* of me!
Oh how my bosom beat and burn'd,
When he from Boston had return'd,
And did relate those wonders wild
Which swell'd the hope of his fond child,
"Dear Sam," said he, "I have in view
A prospect, which I think will do;
'Twill give you *fortune* — ease in life —
A *rank* respectful — and — a wife:
So down to Boston bend your way,
And take a *Shop* without delay —
For scarcely can you walk a street,
But thousand *shoppers* you will meet;
And money there like streams must flow,

Since people all a *shopping* go."
No sooner had my father done
His pleasing speech, than quick I run,
Caught Pony, and set out to see
What Boston folks would do for me.
Ah! surely, Tom, *Dad* was deceiv'd,
And oft I've set me down, and griev'd
That man should be by *follies* rul'd,
And woman still in *fashions* school'd.
What he had seen was a mere hoax—
A *notion* of the Boston folks.
'Tis true they all a shopping go,
But yet 'tis only for a show—
Although from shop to shop they fly,
Believe me, Tom, they seldom buy!
'Tis but to exercise the mind,
To take a *pattern* of each kind,
Until they fill their motley *bags*
So full, you'd think they sold old rags.
I find the *Belles* here *constant* meet,
To talk, to laugh, and walk the street
With shawls neglected, hanging loose,
To shew the *forms* which stays produce—
To bring to view those cheeks of rose,
Which *art* so bounteously bestows.
Thus ev'ry day from year to year,
You view the steps of folly here.
But, Tom, I think I must conclude,
Lest on your patience I intrude:
And only say—if things don't alter,
I must take up the plough, or—halter:
For threescore years, or more, of life,
Will neither fortune give—nor wife.
'Tis not that here's *no trade* at all,
Nor that my *profits*, Tom, are small,
That I complain—no, surely no—
But 'tis, that *half* we make must go
To *Jews*, whose *hearts* are not content,
But when they *shave* at *three per cent*!
That *landlords*, who of wealth possess'd,

Should for their *rents* take all the rest!
Not even leave one cent for those
Who furnish us so *cheap* with clothes.
No, Tom, it will not do, I find,
I have already made my mind
To leave this place, and come to you —
Till which, I haste to bid adieu.

Sam, Boston Weekly Magazine, December 7, 1816

————

[DEAR Jack, I am no more the clown]

MR. EDITOR — I will thank you (if convenient,) to insert in your paper,
the following letter from Tim Fry to his brother, Jack in the country,
which it would hardly be worth while to say "I picked up in the street."

DEAR Jack, I am no more the clown
You thought I was, in *our* town,
For faith, since my arrival here,
The tailors made me look so queer.
You can't conceive my dearest Jack,
Of "Dandies" clothes upon my back,
In fact the ladies all declare:
I am the "beau" of all the fair.
And that of "dandies" (tho' tis true
It can't be said, that there's a few),
I certainly shall "rule the roast"
Tho' faith I am *afeard* almost
To make the trial, for there's one
That swears he will not be out done,
He is a dandy of six feet,
Seen every day in "Market street"
Where too are seen 'most all the fops,
They lounge about the dry goods shops
O could you see him Jack you'd swear,
He does the very image wear
Of that droll "monkey" they display
At ——s, every training day;
His coat is small enough for Tom,
Our little boy I left at home;
With waistcoat cut down in a peak,

And lac'd behind so very sleek,
That like a weasel's body thin,
Is his —— or Mollys rolling pin;
His breeches—may I be so bold,
Would bushels of potatoes hold;
Besides, I'm told the "dandies" wear
The ladies stays, I vow and swear,
I'll never put a pair of these
Upon my back: why faith, they'd squeeze
My marrow bones to jelly nice,
And stop my windpipe in a trice.
You know our Molly? once she tried
To wear a pair when she did ride,
But "*snigs*" she hadn't rode *a bit*,
Before, she fainted in a fit.
Dear Jack, a few more lines I write,
I went to see the play last night:
I was *agoing* in the Pit,
But ——s said it was not fit
For gentlemen, and I must go
With him in No. 1, 1st. row.
So Jack, behold me in my seat,
Dress'd up in "dandy" clothes, so neat;
The play was, "Magpie, and the Maid"
Looked rather old—although 'twas said,
She was *agoing* soon to marry,
A fellow, named Tom, Dick, or Harry,
O Jack, the very devil's in it,
For they did hardly then begin it;
Before the Magpie—Thevish loon,
Flew down, and stole a silver spoon;
It was alive dear, Jack, I swear
It flapp'd its wings when in the air.
And "Forty thieves"—dear Jack I saw,
Which makes me think there is no law;
For apprehending *these* folks here,
Altho' I saw a lawyer near.
And now they let the curtain fall,
And, folks began to scramble all,
I rose and look'd around then said,

Come lets go home and go to bed.
So Jack "good bye, my love to 'Nell'"
Tell her I hope as how she's well,
And write me soon, dear Jack, while I
Am Yours, et cetera. —TIM FRY

Boston Weekly Magazine, February 20, 1819

———

JONATHAN'S JOURNEY TO BOSTON.

The following piece of drollery was handed to us last week, as coming
from Vermont. Whether it is founded on fact, or is an offspring of fancy,
we cannot ascertain. We *guess* that it will appear to some of our readers,
as it does to us, *too long*; but *expect* it will excite a pleasurable smile.

Last Sunday, you know, I was just twenty-one;
On Monday, a *freeman* I rose with the sun,
Resolving to Boston to walk, ride, or run,
Where I never had been to see fashions and fun.

I trudg'd all the way with my clothes on my back,
And a few little notions, snug in my knapsack,
Ten dollars in bills in my pocketbook, whack!
I enclos'd, and my pocket some change did not lack.

As I went along downward, of knowledge a seeker,
The land was more clear'd, barns and houses look'd sleeker,
And the further I went, they charg'd more for their liquor,
Which I found still grew stronger and [made] me *high* quicker.

March 7th P.M. sun half an hour high,
As near as I guess'd 'neath the dark, cloudy sky,
Fam'd Boston appeared with its steeples just by,
And I pass'd o'er the neck, with a wonderstruck eye.

For their houses are high as a dozen of ours
And long, as from our house to grandfather Bower's,
On both sides the road, too, they stand, like great towers,
They must have been built by the old giants' powers.

Here I thought in my soul, there was old Nick to pay,
Such crowds in a hurry were passing each way,
It seem'd from the country was running each *sleigh*,
And folks all from Boston were running away.

I elbow'd along, through fatigue, mud and care,
I cannot tell how, and I cannot tell where,
Till I came to a sign post, rais'd high in the air,
With a sign, that gave notice a tavern was there.

I enter'd the door, for a lodging I ax'd,
For which the bar keeper a pistareen tax'd
I told him 'twas high for my old leather purse—
"Go further," said he, "then, where you may fare worse."

I said I was tir'd, so agreed I would stay,
And down on the nail he demanded the pay,
I paid him, and quickly aside laid my pack,
And in front of the fireplace stood warming my back;

And kept off the heat from those seated around,
Till burnt to a crisp I my pantaloons found.
I marvell'd at that!—for that back log was stone,
The forestick was iron, with *dirt* laid thereon,

They there call it *peat*—it gave a *queer* smell,
Still the fire was as hot as—I don't like to tell.
I now 'gan to stamp and to caper about;
The company set up a giggle and shout;

When, out of the door, what a horrible noise
Arose from the throats of men, women and boys,
From ringing of bells, and from rattling of engines,
And people all running, like fury and vengeance!

I ran with the others, like one in amaze,
And saw a great building all in a light blaze.
I tried to run from it—'twas now light as day—
But such was the crowd, I could not get away.

A great bunch of people, stood, at the fire staring,
Some right in the midst on't were ripping and tearing;
Some goods from the shops and the houses were bearing;
Some crying, some laughing some praying, some swearing.

Now men, with long poles, took the folks by their clothes,
And plac'd a whole snarl all along in two rows,
And made them hand buckets, of leather I s'pose,
And halloo'd, "here water is coming, here goes."

And now from full many a great *lengthy* squirt,
The water in torrents began for to spirt,
Which wet all the buildings — and me to my shirt —
I thought it "would do as much damage as hurt."

But soon I found out, that so great was its power,
It put out the fire, like a great thunder shower,
So they got it subdu'd in the course of an hour,
And homeward again they began for to scour.

But now I found out to my sorrow and cost,
To and fro, here and there, by the crowd being tost,
When many a street, lane and alley I'd cross'd,
That, in the confusion, myself I had lost.

I rambled about in a piteous plight,
Half dead with fatigue, shame, sorrow and fright;
'Till at length I discover'd 'twas growing daylight,
And tow'rd Boston neck one directed me right.

So, after a long and a tedious trudging,
I found out the place, where I paid for my lodging,
And ventur'd the bar room again just to dodge in,
Though the bar keeper took my long absence in dudgeon.

I told him, says I, "let me now have my pack,
And quick to Varmount, I will take myself back."
"Here take it," says he, "give us none of your slack;"
So I took it, and homeward I steered in a crack.

Such being the noise, and confusion in town,
Near father and mother I'll fix myself down,
Take care of the farm—wed *fair* Molly Brown—
And live till I die, a plain good-hearted clown.
Down, down, down   DERRY DOWN.

Anonymous, Ladies' Port Folio, March 25, 1820

————

[In Boston once did A with B contend]

In Boston once did A with B contend,
Till A, hard press'd, chose thus the strife to end;
If Universalism, sir, be true,
Proclaim it not, it may evil do.
Ghent's happy treaty, under flowing sail
Soon reached town, the news with joy all hail;
Quick, wide it flies, B caught it on its wing,
Meets A, looks sad, and talks of other things;
Parting, says B, there's peace for all I hear,
But tell it not 'twill harm some I fear.

Spectator, Universalist Magazine, June 10, 1810

MEN AND WOMEN

William King, silhouette, 1803–10
Courtesy of Historic New England

Boston's a town, polite and debonair,
To which the beaux and beauteous nymphs repair.

— Phillis Wheatley, "An Answer to the Rebus by the Author
of *Poems on Various Subjects, Religious and Moral*" (1773)

I n thus describing the city she had lived in from the age of seven or eight, Phillis Wheatley not only solved but seemingly endorsed the clue provided by one I. B., the anonymous poet to whose rebus she was responding. In its entirety I. B.'s clue ran as follows:

> A town of gaiety and sport,
> Where beaux and beauteous nymphs resort,
> And gallantry doth reign.

If we put the inflated, neoclassical rhetoric aside, what unifies the clue and solution is the idea that relations between men and women in Boston were built on civilized respect and good manners in a world of high style, refinement, and beauty.

At the start of the American Revolution, Abigail Adams (1744–1818), wife of the future second president of the United States, saw these relations in a less celebratory way. In a letter to her husband who was participating in the Continental Congress in Philadelphia, she wrote,

> in the new code of laws which I suppose it will be necessary for you to make, I desire you would remember the ladies and be more generous and favorable to them than your ancestors. Do not put such unlimited power into the hands of the husbands. Remember, all men would be tyrants if they could. If particular care and attention is not paid to the ladies, we are determined to foment a rebellion, and will not hold ourselves bound by any laws in which we have no voice or representation.

Though she was undoubtedly kidding about the rebellion, Adams was serious about the need to reduce the power men wielded over women at a time when girls were treated as intellectual inferiors and wives could not sign legal contracts or control their own money. John Adams (1735–1826) responded in a similarly half-serious tone: "We know better than to repeal our masculine systems. Although they are in full force, you know they are little more than theory. . . . We are obliged to go fair and softly, and, in practice, you know we are the subjects." This undoubtedly affection-ate debate served as prologue to what would be an ongoing, indeed still continuing, consideration of the place of women in a democratic society.

If we put Wheatley's upbeat overview at one end of a spectrum of late-eighteenth-century thinking about male-female relations and Abi-gail Adams's view at the other, the range of views between them suggests what we can expect to encounter in poems on this topic from the 1790s on. Fueled by the force of revolutionary upheaval, the period covered by this anthology saw the first powerful articulations of modern feminism. Following—and, in the notable case of Judith Sargent Murray, to some ex-tent anticipating—the radical insights of Mary Wollstonecraft (1759–97), Boston thinkers in the 1790s and 1800s waded into this debate. Hannah Webster Foster (1758–1840), a resident of Brighton, published *The Co-quette*, a novel that exposes the limited options available to women, here in 1797. Susanna Rowson, who wrote *Charlotte Temple* (1791), the most popular novel in America before *Uncle Tom's Cabin* (1851), moved to Bos-ton in 1796 and performed in her own play, *Slaves in Algiers* (1794), at the Federal Street Theatre. Its saucy epilogue includes the following taunt: "Women were born for universal sway; Men to adore, be silent, and obey." And Murray—novelist, essayist, poet, and playwright—made the case for women's emotional and intellectual equality two years before English feminist Wollstonecraft published her *Vindication of the Rights of Women* (1792). Indeed, in her first published essay, "Desultory Thoughts upon the Utility of Encouraging a Degree of Self-Complacency, Especially in Fe-male Bosoms" (1784), Murray insisted on the importance of cultivating self-esteem in girls, while in subsequent essays she argued for women's intellectual and emotional equality, upgrading female education, and training girls for economic self-reliance.

In the poems collected here, different points of view are represented. Several feature strong, clever, and determined female voices. "On the CHOICE of a HUSBAND" (*Massachusetts Magazine*, August 1790) pres-ents a worldly-wise speaker who offers a catalogue of men to avoid, from the "changeable fry" to the "dogmatick elf," from the "fluttering fop" to the "guttling [gorging] sot." In a colloquial style, the speaker urges women to shun men who are "bedup'd by their [own] passions." While her final advice, that women seek out wise and virtuous mates, is conventional enough, her overview of the range of bad choices out there creates a clear if also comic sense of the dangers facing young women. Similarly cautious voices can be heard in "The MODEST WISH of SUSAN, the BREECHES MAKER" and "THE MAN TO MY MIND."

Faced with the prospect of a bad marriage—seemingly guaranteed by the laws that governed spousal rights and the norms that regulated spousal relations—the extraordinarily high-spirited and self-reliant speaker in the 1794 poem "LINES *Written by a Lady who was questioned respecting her inclination to marry*" scorns wedlock as a system of oppression. Animated by the spirit of the French Revolution, she defies "tyrannical systems and modes" of matrimony and embraces the life of an "Old Maid," claiming her place as a member of the "republic of freedom and ease." The extract from Robert Treat Paine's "The Ruling Passion"—included here as "The Old-Maid" from the March 4, 1804, issue of the *Boston Weekly Magazine*—takes a more conventional view of single women, seeing them as coy, aging, self-defeating, and "sour" misanthropists.

In "A HINT TO A FRIEND" (*Something*, December 16, 1809), a young woman is urged to be less interested in fashion, while in *"Advice to the young Ladies of* Boston" (*Gentlemen and Ladies' Town and Country Magazine*, May 1789), women are advised to avoid both pride and coquetry by cultivating inner beauty, "a mild address, [and] an unaffected air." Opposite cautionary advice to young men can be found in "LOOK BEFORE YOU LEAP" and "SONG. I courted a girl that I long wished to marry." In the former, the speaker avoids marrying a pregnant young woman; in the latter, the speaker realizes that the woman he has been courting can only be attracted by the lure of wealth. Pessimism vies with misogyny in *"Lines Spoken Extempore to a Lady, on being asked what this world is like"* which sees the world as a prison in which one is chained by or to women! As a group, these poems confirm the difficulties of finding an acceptable spouse.

Susanna Rowson's "SIMILE. Passion is like the base narcotic flower" —which ran in the August 27, 1803, issue of the *Boston Weekly Magazine* —compares the scent of a rose to the effect of love. Just as the rose's scent lingers after the flower dies, love endures after death. While Rowson concludes with the "pure love" of the rose, the earlier description of passion as a "base narcotic flower" dominates the poem. Unlike love, passion's "baleful poison" "benumbs the sense." While love's perfume lingers after death, passion's "nefarious power" is deceptive and ephemeral. Speaking of passion, don't confuse the brevity of "CROSSES" (*Boston Weekly Magazine*, April 7, 1804) with simplicity. Depending on which meanings of the word "cross" you think are at play, it can be read as advocating either frequent sex or frequent arguments in marriage!

Attraction and desire animate both "A LADY, who lately attempted" and "ENQUIRY." In the former, the speaker falls in love with a man she has been trying to draw; in the latter, the speaker describes the thrill of holding a lover's hand. In a radically different mood, virulent misogyny rears its head in the epitaph (reprinted, from earlier publication in London, in the November 5, 1803, issue of the *Boston Weekly Magazine*) that begins, "Here lies the quintessence of noise and strife, / Or in one word—here lies a scolding wife." It's interesting to note that this insulting, foreign poem (featured in Thomas Caldwell's *Collection of Epitaphs and Inscriptions*, published in London in 1791) inspired a passionate response from a local reader. His poem, which ran one week later in the same magazine, begins by addressing an ill-treated wife named Isabel and then offers a defense of women in her situation. This strain of pro- and anti-woman rhetoric climaxes here in the sparring of Ned Megrims (pseudonym) and his adversaries in the *Boston Weekly Magazine* in the late 1810s. For example, when Megrims compares the seemingly sweet kisses of women to the guilty kiss of Judas in "WOMAN" (November 15, 1817), Mora (pseudonym) responds two weeks later in "ANSWER TO THE LINES ENTITLED 'WOMAN,' SIGNED, NED MEGRIMS," by noting that Judas was a man! In response to Megrims's observation that seemingly demure wives enjoy gossiping about their "friends" especially if they can destroy their reputations, Mora notes that when women "fall," they fall because men have "snared" them. At a time when women's potential was widely debated and when social and familial roles were in flux, the dynamism of these changes manifested in politics, economics, education, and—as these poems demonstrate—in the heartfelt, often quarrelsome, and usually pointed outpourings of Boston's citizen poets.

A RECIPE FOR THE LADIES, *Or, advice how to get a Husband*

If you wish to get married, Enitia[†] attend,
You ask'd my advice, I give it, my Friend;
The girl whose good nature, is just like the Sun,
Beaming bright on the world, yet confined to none,
May saunter through life, till Forty, or more,
With Fops who admire, and Fools that adore;
Then find her mistake, and lamenting her fate,
Reform, and grow grave, but rather too late;
Suffice it then Madam, politely to hint,
If you *alter a little*, (the Deuce will be in't)
(And all my predictions, I'm sure must be wrong)
Unless that you're married, before it is long.
Exchange my good friend, for a spice of Disdain,
That warmth of affection, which kills a poor swain,
Renounce your gay smiles, assume a dread Frown,
Only simper a trifle, and catch half the town,
Then pick who you please, (but leaving out merit)
Some Buck, or gay lad, sweet fellow of spirit,
Will please you the most—as a partner for life,
And faith you will make him an excellent Wife.

Altamont, Gentlemen and Ladies' Town and Country Magazine, February 1789

[†]*Enitia*: older or elder sister.

————

Advice to the young Ladies of Boston

Ye lovely nymphs of Boston's beauteous race,
Let no false shews[†] your native charms disgrace.
Ape not the vain Coquette, too kind or rude,
Nor imitate the stiff dissembling prude.
A heart to pride unknown, a smile sincere,
A mild address, an unaffected air;
Will make mankind your pleasing worth approve,
And gently fix the lasting chain of love.

Anonymous, Gentlemen and Ladies' Town and Country Magazine, May 1789

[†]*shews*: shows.

On the CHOICE of a HUSBAND.

Assist me, ye Nine,
Whilst the Youth I define,
With whom I in wedlock wou'd class;
And ye blooming fair,
Lend a listening ear,
To approve of the man as you pass.

Not the changeable fry
Who love, nor know why,
But follow bedup'd by their passions;
Such vot'ries as these
Are like waves of the seas,
And steer'd by their own inclinations.

The hectoring blade,
How unfit for the maid,
Where meekness and modesty reigns!
Such a thundering bully,
I'll speak against truly,
Whatever I get for my pains.

Not the dogmatick elf,
Whose great all is himself,
Whose alone ipse dixit† is law;
What a figure he'll make,
How like Momus† he'll speak,
With a sneering burlesque, a pshaw! pshaw!

Nor the covetuous wretch,
Whose heart's at full stretch
To gain an inordinate treasure;
Him leave with the rest
And such mortals detest,
Who sacrifice life without measure.

The fluttering fop,
How empty his top!
Nay, but some call him coxcomb, I trow;
But 'tis losing your time,
He's not half worth a rhyme,
Let the fag ends of prose bind his brow.

The guttling† sot,
What a conduit his throat!
How beastly and vicious his life!
Where drunkards prevail,
Whose families feel,
Much more an affectionate wife.

One character yet
I with sorrow repeat,
And Oh! that the number were less;
'Tis the blasphemous crew,
What a pattern they'll shew
To their hapless and innocent race.

Let Wisdom then shine
In the youth that is mine,
While Virtue his footsteps impress;
Such I'd chuse for my mate,
Whether sooner or late,
Tell me, Ladies, what think you of this?

Eusebia, *Massachusetts Magazine*, August 1790.

---

†*ipse dixit*: he himself said (Latin); *Momus*: in Greek mythology, a god associated with satire, mockery and censure; *guttling*: eating or drinking greedily.

―――――

The MODEST WISH of SUSAN, the BREECHES MAKER

BESIDE a lamp, besmear'd with oil,
Sue toiling sat for riches;
Her aching heart, a husband fill'd;
Her lap, a pair of breeches.

ı me"! with feeble voice, she cry'd,
    ῳhile sighs oft rose with stitches,
"Ah me! and must I live a maid;
And only *make* the breeches:

"Ye Gods"! then rais'd to heav'n her eyes—
"O! grant my wish, soon, which is,
A husband young, a kind, good man;
And let me *wear* the breeches."

CLEON, Massachusetts Magazine, February 1791

LINES *Written by a Lady, who was questioned respecting her inclination to marry*

With an heart light as cork, and a mind free as air,
Unshackled I'll live and I'll die, I declare;
No ties shall perplex me, no fetters shall bind,
That innocent freedom that dwells in my mind.
At liberty's spring, such draughts I've imbib'd,
That I hate all the doctrines by wedlock prescrib'd.
Its laws of obedience could never suit me,
My spirit's too lofty, my thoughts are too free.
Like an haughty republic my heart with disdain
Views the edicts of Hymen and laughs at his chain,
Abhors his tyrannical systems and modes,
His bastiles, his shackles, his maxims and codes;
Inquires why women consent to be tools,
And calmly conform to such rigorous rules;
Inquires in vain, for no reasons appear,
Why matrons should live in subjection and fear.
But round freedom's fair standard I've rallied and paid,
A vow of allegiance to die an old maid.
Long live the republic of freedom and ease,
May its subjects live happy and do as they please.

Anonymous [Judith Sargent Murray?], Massachusetts Magazine, September 1794

Lines Spoken Extempore to a Lady,
on being asked what this world is like

The *world* is a *prison*, in every respect,
    Whose *walls* are the *heavens* in common—
The *jailor* is *sin*, the *prisoners*, *men*,
    And the *fetters*, nothing but *women*.

Anonymous, Nightingale, May 19, 1796

————

SIMILE. [PASSION is like the base narcotic flower]

Passion is like the base narcotic flower,
    That flaunts its scarlet bosom to the day;
And when exerting its nefarious power,
    Benumbs the sense, and steals the strength away.

In the gay morn attractive to the eye,
    Its thin leaves flutter in the wanton wind;
But e'er the sun declines, will fade and die,
    While still its baleful poison lurks behind.

But Love! pure Love! the human soul pervading,
    Is like the musk rose, scenting summer's breath;
It charms when budding, in its prime; and fading,
    Will even yield a rich perfume in death.

SR [Susanna Rowson], Boston Weekly Magazine, August 27, 1803

————

EPITAPH. [HERE lies the quintessence of noise and strife]

HERE lies the quintessence of noise and strife,
Or in one word—here lies a scolding wife:
Had not death took her when her mouth was shut,
He dar'd not for his ears have touch'd the slut.

Anonymous, Boston Weekly Magazine November 5, 1803.

[OH, envy'd happiness! said Isabel]

Messrs. GILBERT & DEAN,

If you think the enclosed lines worthy of a place, please to publish them, as a contrast to the Epitaph on "A Scolding Wife," which appeared in your last Saturday's Magazine.

OH, envy'd happiness! said Isabel,
    As chance an accidental look had giv'n,
While Florimet caress'd his Florimel,
    And fondly call'd her, the "best gift of Heav'n."

Oh, envy'd happiness! Not mine to know,
    Said Isabel; hymeneal bonds to me,
Are lasting chains, to tyranny and woe,
    And death's kind hand alone can set me free.

Could I *one word* of tenderness receive,
    From him who was the idol of my love,
I'd cease to murmur, I would yet believe,
    That my submission would his pity move,

But ah, submission! I have try'd thy pow'r;
    Too long I've rested on thy feeble aid,
To greet my wishes with *one* social hour,
    When nuptial grief should not that hour invade.

But 'tis in vain! I'm only doom'd to see,
    That calm submission aggravates my grief,
Prolongs my woes, extends my misery,
    And hides in shades, a shadow of relief.

Ah, cruel destiny! why was I born,
    In unremitting warfare to engage;
To be the object of contemptuous scorn,
    The suff'ring subject of a tiger's rage?

Cold, and unfeeling, in his *sober* hours,
    Few as they are, my tyrant's hated voice
Thunders his will, while on his forehead lours,
    The scowling omen of tumultuous noise.

But this, e'en this, is *music* to the peal
      Of curses, bellow'd up from the abyss,
Of that foul ocean, where the senses reel,
      And pitch from reason's seat, in drunkenness.

Here, for complaint, would be abundant cause,
      But griefs, still heavier, wreck my sinking frame;
If this were all, here would I gladly pause,
      But deeper baseness, stamps my husband's shame.

The man, the guard of woman was ordain'd,
      And feeble woman needs his kindly aid;
Then shall his sanguin'd hands, be basely stain'd,
      By female wounds, *his* cruelty has made!

This too I've borne, and this I still must bear;
      With blows dishearten'd, and with wrongs oppress'd,
I sigh my anguish, to the midnight air,
      And breathe the lab'rings of my tortur'd breast.

In piteous accents, thus complaind the wife,
      Whose furrow'd cheek had lost its rosy bloom;
Her youth and spirit, by domestic strife,
      Transform'd to age, and melancholy gloom.

Ah, Isabella! could I give relief,
      Could I by searching, find the just decree,
To guard thy rights, I'd fly to stop thy grief:
      But—Isabella! THERE'S NO LAW FOR THEE.

Pacificus, Boston Weekly Magazine, November 12,1803

———

[The Old-Maid]

Messrs. Gilbert & Dean,
THE following picture of an *Old-Maid*, is extracted from [Robert Treat]
Paine's poem, "The Ruling Passion." I have read it to my sister, who I fear
will be one of the "Order," for if a young man happens to take her by the
hand, she withdraws it with as much velocity, as a star shoots . . .

BUT, see, what form, so sprig'd, behoop'd, and sleek,
With modern head-dress on a block antique,
Trips through the croud, and ogling all who pass,
Stares most demurely thro' an *Op'ra glass*!
Sunk in the wane, she courts the gay parade—
A belle of PLATO's AGE—a sweet OLD MAID.
While *liv'd* her beauty, (for 'tis now a *ghost!*)
The fair one's envy, and the fopling's toast,
What slaughter'd hearts by her fierce eye-beams fell,
Let fiction's brokers—bards and tombstones tell.
Fled are the charms, which graced that ivory brow;
Where smiled a *dimple*, gapes a *wrinkle* now:
And e'en that pouting lip, where whilom grew
The mellow peach-down, and the ruby's hue,
No more can trance the ear with sweeter sounds,
Than fairies warble on enchanted grounds!
    Now, hapless nymph! she wakes from dreams of bliss,
The knee adoring, and the stolen kiss,
And for the Persian worship of the eye,
Meets the arch simper of the *mimic* sigh.
Still she resolves her empire to regain,
And rifles fashion, tortures art, to reign.
Oft at the ball, she flaunts, in flowers so gay,
She seems DECEMBER in the robes of MAY;
And oft more coy, coquettes, behind her fan,
That odious monster—dear, sweet creature, Man!
    At length grown ugly, past the aid of gold;
And, spite of essences and *rouge*, grown old;
Each softer passion yields to pride's control,
And sour misanthropy usurps her soul.
Now, first on Man, the spleeny gossip rails,
Arraigns his justice, and his taste assails;
Till, as her *tea's* exhausted fragrance flies,
Her wit evaporates—her scandal dies.
Yet still invidious of the art to bless,
She blasts the joys, she lingers to possess;
And, while on HYMEN'S bridal rites she sneers,
Her pillow trickles with repentant tears.
While thus, to all her sex's pleasures dead,
She vents her rage on ADAM'S guilty head,

Who rather chose, than lose his *rib* for life,
To have the *crooked member* made a wife;
From waking wo to vision'd bliss she flies,
And dreams of raptures, which her fate denies.
The tender flame, which warm'd her youthful mind,
By AFFECTATION'S mawkish rules confin'd,
Though quench'd its heat, illumes with many a ray,
The tedious evening of her fading day;
And though unknown, unnotic'd, and unblest,
Still suns th' IMPASSIVE WINTER of her breast.

Robert Treat Paine, *Boston Weekly Magazine*, March 3, 1804

————

CROSSES.

If *crosses* in wedlock are not seen to please,
The man that is married can have *little ease*;
Then right hand and left hand at a wedding are giv'n,
The *cross* first beginneth before God and Heav'n;
One *crosses* the other by mutual consent,
O'er the face—*cross* the lips, with a kiss it is meant.
No wonder if *crosses* continue for life—
The man that loves most, will the most *cross* his wife.

Anonymous, *Boston Weekly Magazine*, April 1804

————

[Thy manly face I strove to hit]

A LADY, who lately attempted to delineate the features of her lover, in the midst of her employment, relinquished the pencil, and taking up the pen, addressed to him the following affectionate compliment,

Thy manly face I strove to hit,
My art thy graces foil;
Short of success, yet loath to quit,
My hand renews the toil.

Love's laughing God my sketches spied,
And, with his sharpest dart,
My inexpressive skill supplied,
And grav'd thee in my heart.

Anonymous, *Boston Weekly Magazine*, June 23, 1804

ENQUIRY.

When her eyes are softly telling,
    What your heart must understand;
When you see her bosom swelling,
    As you slightly touch her hand;
Should affection prompt the action,
    Can you decide which most is blest;
By the fingers soft contraction,
    The hand which presses, or is prest?

Anonymous, Boston Weekly Magazine, September 1, 1804

———

THE WISH

I WISH not for riches, I wish not for fame;
The first is mere pelf, and the second a name.
In ambition's fierce stream I wish not to be carried—
What wish you for then? Why, I wish to be married.

Anonymous, Polyanthos, January 1, 1806

———

Impromptu on the Marriage of Capt. Foot, with Miss Patten.[†]

MAY the union cemented this morning at matin,
    Be blissful and crown'd with abundant of fruit.
May the *Foot* ever closely adhere to the *Patten*;
    The *Patten* for ever stick close to the *Foot*!
And tho' pattens are used in moist dirty weather,
    May their journey thro' life be unclouded and clean,
May they long *fit* each other—and, moving together,
    May only one *sole* still be cherish'd between.

Anonymous, The Fly; or, Juvenile Miscellany, March 19, 1806

[†]*Patten*: a shoe with a raised sole that keeps one's feet above wet ground.

THE MAN TO MY MIND.

They tell me 'tis quite in the fashion to marry,
And wonder I'm single — I'm not in a hurry;
I will never be wed until I can find,
In ev'ry respect, the man to my mind.
Believe me, of offers I've had not a few
From the witty, rich, handsome, and affable too;
But even with all these attractions combin'd,
It appears I've not found the man to my mind.
From such it may seem I am rather unfair,
And because I am young, that I need not despair;
But answer me this, with a friendship that's kind,
Is it right I should wed — but the man to my mind?
The miser I hate, for he worships his gold;
And profligates too, their affections are cold;
Yet a fondness that's foolish — as the man that's unkind,
I never could call him the man to my mind.
The man I could wed, should we happen to meet,
Must not be a fribble, a fop — but discreet;
The coxcomb I hate, for he ne'er can be kind;
His ways are not suited at all to my mind.

Anonymous, Emerald, June 6, 1807

————

A PARODY.

YE fair sprightly maids, who lament that your power,
Too transient, secures but the boast of an hour;
Attend to my council, nor blush to be taught,
That Good Humour may charm whom your beauty ne'er caught.

In a spotless white robe, like the feminine dress,
The Poets paint Angels on errands of peace,
Let your angel attire, emblematic be seen,
Of a heart unpolluted, and temper serene.

Be the chief of your study the duties of life,
To excel in the arts which embellish a wife;
With good nature refuse, or discreetly be kind;
And nurse with attention, the charms of the mind.

Let your wit never wound with a smart repartee;
Be your converse complacent, engaging and free;
As companions, you then may COMMAND that respect,
Which would FLY FROM YOUR WIT, and give place to neglect.

Thus the good temper'd Girl, that regard shall insure,
Which the bloom of her Beauty would never secure;
And when once so acquired, it will ever survive,
For the art which obtained it, will keep it alive.

Anonymous, Useful Cabinet, January 1, 1808

Epigram [That ladies are the softer sex]

That ladies are the softer sex 'tis said;
True, sir—they're soft in heart, in hand and head.

Anonymous, Ordeal, May 20, 1809

A HINT TO A FRIEND.

By every object we behold,
    From infinite to nought,
Some moral lesson we are told,
    Or some new feeling taught.

Yes, nature bountiful as free,
    If carefully we scan,
Exhibits every thing we see,
    To be the guide of man.

A moth hover'd round us, while Julia in pain,
    Still follow'd its fluttering maze;
From the flame she attempted to save it in vain,
    She wept, as it scorch'd in the blaze.

Ah Julia! forgive, if affectionate care,
    Too strong a resemblance presumes:
The moth is the female that's dazzled by glare,
    And fashion the blaze that consumes.

Anonymous, Something, December 16, 1809

TO MY FRIEND.

No simple, gay, fantastic girl,
    In love shall e'er my heart entwine;
Nor will I homage pay to wealth,
    Nor yet will bow at beauty's shrine.

But the fair maid whom nature's blest
    With wisdom, far beyond her years;
Who o'er the charms of innocence
    The attractive robe of virtue wears:

Whose graceful form and modest mein,
    Has with them dignity combin'd;
Whose wealth is in her knowledge stor'd;
    Whose richest beauty's in her mind;

And who abroad's politely gay,
    Cheerful at home, with ease;
Whose gentle manners always strive,
    Her every friend to please,

I'd make my choice—and to her worth
    Pay the just tribute due;
And prize her far above the wealth
    Of India, or Peru.

For, when with troublous cares oppress'd,
    To her I'd them impart;
Who, with endearing smiles of love,
    Would *lull* my restive heart.

If I were weary—then would I,
    Within her guardian arms,
Lull me in safety to repose,
    Secure from threat'ning harms.

If I were ill—her watchful care
    Would *lull* my throbbing breast;
Lull every tumult of the soul,
    And *lull* my pains to rest.

And should the tongue of slander dare
    Asperse my valued name;
Her chaster breath would *lull* its rage,
    And vindicate my fame.

With such a shield encompass'd round,
    I'd *lull* a world of care;
Lull my fond hopes — my fears, too, *lull*,
    And *lull* me in despair.

B.R., Something, May 5, 1810

————

SONG. [I courted a girl that I long wished to marry]

I courted a girl that I longed wished to marry,
And thought if I had her, I never should rue;
So shy did she seem I thought hope would miscarry,
As her only reply was, "indeed it wont do."

Confound it said I, what a matter is this,
Am I doom'd other ways to pursue?
Nor thought till that moment that money was bliss,
And nothing but dollars would do.

So I stole to my hoard that was easily tried,
And took for a ticket a few,
Then hasten'd to the place* where the prizes are sold,
Just to see what the dollars would do.

So throng'd were the door, I could scarcely get in
Yet I clumsily forc'd my way through,
And want of politeness appear'd as no din,
As I'd nothing but dollars in view.

In three weeks at most, I'd a capital prize,
Quite enough my fond hopes to renew,
And shew'd the BANK NOTES to those beautiful eyes,
Just to try if she'd say "it won't do."

But what most of all has increas'd my delight,
And with pleasure I own it is true,
For I *never since* heard her by day or by night,
Make use of the words, "it won't do."

Anonymous, Scourge, August 28, 1811

Gilbert & Dean, Exchange Building [original note].

———

LOOK BEFORE YOU LEAP. A TRUE STORY

How glow'd my breast when first I walked,
    With C.P. then not quite fifteen,
To mark her meekness while she talk'd,
    Tho' not with faith, of things unseen.

Sweet innocence betray'd each look,
    That o'er her dimpled beauty shone,
When as her timid hand I took,
    To press or speak of days to come.

Yet I unconscious of her love,
    With heavenly passive influence mild,
Wish'd but one proof, when lo, to prove,
    I viewed her sharp, she was with ——.

Anonymous, Scourge, October 3, 1811

———

SINGLE BLESSEDNESS.
Messrs. Editors,
The appearance of one of our Club, in your last, has encouraged me to
offer the enclosed; if it meet your approbation, by inserting it you will
much oblige yours. H.S.

I sing of joys perfect and pure,
    Of pleasures we bachelors share;
Of happiness solid and sure,
    Devoid of all trouble and care.

When we rise from our bed at the dawn,
    We rove as we list unrestrain'd,
As free as the zephyrs of morn,
    And laugh at the fools who're enchain'd.

In a cot where good cheer doth entice,
    Where peace and content reigns serene,
(Except a *black tabby* for mice,)
    No *female* was ever yet seen.

Nor is heard the melodious notes,
    Of "family music" so fine,
When a score of squalling young throats,
    In concert harmonious join.

Nor the breeze so benignant of love,
    Transformed to the whirlwind of rage,
Blows furious from deary, my dove,
    And defies all attempts to assuage.

With the bliss, that this truth must attend
    When the clouds of misfortune abound,
With scarcely a penny to spend;
    And a brood almost starving around.

These cares shall ne'er enter our cot,
    Independent we swear to remain,
Keep aloof from the hymenial knot,
    Nor be bound by an apron-string-chain.

At eve we'll the pleasure enjoy,
    Of a home freed from woman and woe,
With a book and segar we'll employ
    The moments of time as they go.

Then here's to the state "single blessedness,"
    The perfect elysium below,
For wedlock's a state of wretchedness,
    And conjugal bliss is all show.

H.S., *Boston Weekly Magazine*, June 14, 1817

MATRIMONY.

A Reply to "Single Blessedness," in [the] last Magazine

Of heavenly pleasures I sing,
    Man's greatest enjoyment below,
Those delights which from conjugal happiness spring,
    Which bachelors never can know.

How dreary and lonesome is life,
    Though plenty and friends smile around,
Without the enlivening smile of a wife,
    'Tis all but a bubble or sound.

For what are the comforts of home?
    With all that the senses can crave,
If woman be absent, ('twere better to roam)
    'Tis cheerless and dull as the grave.

Then let mine be some rural retreat,
    Where all may contentment discern;
A wife's cheering welcome at night let me meet,
    As I home from my labours return.

Then here's *matrimony* forever,
    On which life's enjoyment depends,
To fulfill my duty shall be my endeavor,
    At home "with wife, children and friends."

Ronald, *Boston Weekly Magazine*, June 21, 1817

———

WOMAN.

WOMAN can kiss, and kiss, and kiss so sweet!
And so could Judas—kisses of deceit.
The guilty kiss his traitor soul beli'd;
So under smiles and kisses women hide
The rottenness within, and veil deceit
Under embraces kind, and kisses sweet.
A woman's temper is an April day;
For a short time the cheering sunbeams play,

Then storms and winds succeed—and then again
The sunbeams smile, and then again 'tis rain.
Now comes a sudden squall, and now a storm,
And now 'tis cold—and now again 'tis warm.
Wind, clouds, and sun, appear to beat strife,
Just like a peevish, smiling, scolding wife.
From the young, forward tit, whose bosom springs
At thoughts of love, affection, and such things;
From matrons comely, past the prime of life,
From the young fawning, smiling, tender wife,
From wither'd maids, whose hopes of love are o'er,
In doubt to join the church or fish for more;
To the decrepid, wrinkled, toothless dame,
A neighbour's reputation is fair game.
Ask the demure, the prim, the pious wife
What gives the greatest pleasure in this life?
And if for once, without her usual art,
She freely gives the answer of her heart,
She'll say, "A sister's fall, where I have stood;
A friend's fair fame destroy'd, while mine is good."

Ned Megrims, Boston Weekly Magazine, November 15, 1817

———

ANSWER TO THE LINES ENTITLED 'WOMAN,' SIGNED, NED MEGRIMS.

"Woman can kiss, and kiss, and kiss so sweet!
And so could Judas—kisses of deceit."
"A woman's temper is an April day,"
Where squalls, and storms, and even *sunbeams* play.
To maid, to wife, to matron, toothless dame,
"A neighbour's reputation is fair game."
And if for once, without her usual art,
The prim, the pious wife' breathes forth her heart,
She bids a "sister's fall" *her* triumph raise,
The blacken'd fame of "friends" *her* virtues praise.
But man! O noble man! With *honour* crown'd,
His brighter merits, *talents*, should be own'd,
His fame extoll'd, his *very thoughts* applauded,

And with the meed of praise each act rewarded.
Judas comes first—*Judas!* Yes, even *he*—a *man*—
Without whose *kisses of deceit*,
Quite at a loss you were your line to plan;
Naught had you to compare with woman's "kiss so sweet."
'Tis pity, sure, that *man*, already plac'd
So high beyond our reach for talents rare,
That we, (poor souls) must feel still more disgrac'd,
Indebted e'en to *him*, for wherewith to compare
The lines, by which our characters you've trac'd.
Seest thou the cloud on woman's April day?
'Tis *man's* majestic frown which bears such sway,
That woman's heart, not like *his*—*nobly hard*,
Melts into tears—and every drop that falls,
Bears the reflection only of *his* squalls;
Yet *even more*, he claims our thanks, our warm regard.
For how could wife or matron, maid or dame,
Find reputations they might think fair game,
Or wife so prim rejoice at sister's fall
Mid snares, had *man* not *kindly* laid them all.
First blotted reputation by *his* art,
And built the stage where slander plays her part.
Still we look up to his superior pow'rs,
The *subjects his*—the *handling only*—ours.
Yet cease this strain; if 'Megrims' will confess
He chose the *base* alone of woman's race,
And kindly draw discriminating lines
Between where malice glooms, and merit shines,
I'll frankly own, there even are *some men*,
Whose thoughts, words, deeds,
Could *well* be *spoken*, *thought*, and *done again*.

Mora, *Boston Weekly Magazine*, November 29, 1817

———

A TALE.

SOME, who are friends to marriage, say
It keeps young men from wandering astray;
By this, from dissipation they escape;
By this are kept from many a wicked scrape.

This strange assertion brings into my head
A story which I've somewhere heard or read.
A sailor, once, elate with grog or pride,
To show his skill in horsemanship, would ride:
And bawling, 'topsails up, and mizen down!'
Scampered like Satan forward through the town.
The horse, who ne'er had heard a sailor roar,
Nor had a sailor on his back before,
Threw up his heels, most wickedly uncivil,
And gallop'd onwards like the very devil.
Th' undaunted tar relinquishes the rein,
Seizing, with both his hands, the flowing mane,
Draws both his heels close to the horse's sides,
And, Gilpin† like, through shouting crowds he rides:
'The man is run away with!' cried the crowd;
'Hip! Hoi she sails!' the sailor bawls as loud;
While 'stop him! stop him!' was the general yell,
He cooly turn'd his quid, and cried, 'all's well!'
Thus on he rode; but stumbling in the course,
Keel upward went at length both man and horse;
Over each other in the dust they roll'd,
A woful sight, and piteous to behold.
'I'll teach the prancing rascal how to sail,
I'll *ballast* him against another gale,'
Exclaim'd the sailor; then about his tail,
Maliciously he tied a ponderous stone,
And mounting up the horse again, urg'd on.
But vain now was the whip, in vain the rein,
The sailor's roaring oaths were all in vain;
The steed, so fiery and wild before,
Now heeded not the whip, the rein or roar;
His courage fail'd, his spirits too were gone,
When at his tail he felt the heavy stone.
Now listen to the moral of my story,
Which, gen'rously I haste to lay before ye.
Youth is a noble, headstrong, fiery steed;
Love gives the rein, and passion takes the lead:
Wildly through pleasure's flowery paths he flies,
Anxious to know, to taste, and realize,
Each sweet, intoxicating joy of life—

Till, *ballasted* by that vile thing, a wife,
His courage droops, his manly fire is lost,
His noble nature humbled in the dust;
He sorrowfully drudges to his grave,
A doting ideot, a weak woman's slave.

Ned Megrims, Boston Weekly Magazine, November 29, 1817

†*Gilpin*: John Gilpin, the subject of William Cowper's "The Diverting History of John Gilpin" (1782), is separated from the rest of his family when he loses control of his horse.

————

[What's become of Ned Megrims would any one know]

What's become of Ned Megrims would any one know,
I will tell what I heard, tho' perhaps 'tis not so;
I heard that one day, he fell ill of the spleen,
When a fit of the blue devils, also, set in;
He foam'd at the mouth and rav'd with his tongue,
And curs'd maids and widows and wives old and young.
The women all fled at the sound of his voice,
And even the men were alarm'd at the noise.
So they call'd in a Doctor they happen'd to meet,
Who was walking, along, up and down in the street,
And show'd him to Ned — quite a stranger 'twas thought —
For 'twas Reason herself in the Doctor's old coat.
How well it became her, I can't stop to tell,
For poor Mr. Megrims was terribly ill.
Now the doctor walk'd up with a very grave look,
And lifted his wand o'er his head as he spoke,
Come out of him all ye foul spirits, he said,
They heard the command and departed from Ned.
Restor'd to his senses — Ned call'd in the sex,
That he'd spent all his talents to plague and perplex;
And when he'd collected them all round his bed,
With his eyes full of tears he look'd up and he said,
"Sweet souls, the delight and the comfort of men,
I have done you much wrong with my tongue and my pen,
But now I repent" — Alas! his voice shook,
And he ne'er spoke again — but he gave such a look

Of repentance and love, as he bowed to his fate,
That they cri'd "Live Megrims!" but oh! 'twas too late.

Anonymous, Boston Weekly Magazine, January 16, 1819

————

WOMAN.

Gone from her cheek is the summer bloom,
And her breath hath lost all its faint perfume,
And the gloss hath dropped from her golden hair,
And her forehead is pale, though no longer fair.
And the Spirit that sat on her soft blue eye,
Is struck with cold mortality;
And the smile that played on her lip hath fled,
And every grace hath now left the dead.
Like slaves they obeyed her in height of power,
But left her all in her wintry hour;
And the crowds that swore for her love to die,
Shrank from the tone of her last sad sigh —
And this is *Man's* fidelity.
'Tis *Woman* alone, with a firmer heart,
Can see all these idols of life depart,
And love the more: and sooth, and bless
Man in his utter wretchedness.

Anonymous, Boston Weekly Magazine, March 6,1819

————

LADIES' DRESS.

HOW many dresses ladies wear,
In all of which pride has a share.
The morning dishabille appears
And answers well for household cares;
But more complete and full attire,
Their walks and afternoons require.
To worship the Great God of heaven,
More richly dress'd one day in seven;
But when in parties they appear,
A finer dress they choose to wear;
And when to ball-rooms they advance,

And join the lively, giddy dance,
More gaudy dress becomes the scene,
Where sashes wave and spangles gleam.
But soon the sprightly hours are past,
For pleasures cannot always last.
A cold ensues and sickness comes,
Disorder seats upon the lungs;
A chamber dress is now put on,
Nor chang'd at morn or evening sun.
But mortal sickness soon is o'er,
The lady needs but one dress more.

B., *Universalist Magazine*, January 22, 1820

POLITICS

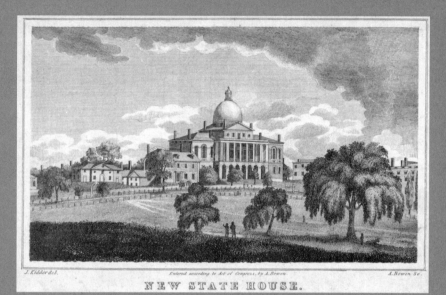

Abel Bowen, new State House, 1825
Courtesy of the Boston Public Library, Print Department

On January 1, 1831, a decade after the terminal point for poems included in this collection, William Lloyd Garrison (1805–79) began to publish his abolitionist magazine the *Liberator* from offices in Boston's Merchants Hall. At a time when poetry served multiple purposes that would later shift to other genres, it is not surprising that the prospectus Garrison placed on the first page of his first issue was written in verse. Called "THE SALUTATION," it is spoken in the voice of the paper itself:

> My name is "LIBERATOR"! I propose
> To hurl my shafts at freedom's deadliest foes!
> My task is hard—for I am charged to save
> *Man from his brother!*—to redeem the slave!

Where the romantic poet aims for ambiguity, subjectivity, and moodiness, this poem strides up to readers, grabs them by their shoulders, looks them in the eyes, and declares its purpose and point. It goes on to ask a series of rhetorical questions and use the implied answers to outline the abolitionist arguments that will animate the magazine for its succeeding, decades-long run: "Art thou a parent? . . . Art thou a brother? . . . Art thou a lover?" Whichever of these identity categories you fit into, asserts the voice of the magazine, you have particular reasons to abhor the slave system.

Moving forward from the early 1830s, Garrison's inclination to deploy poetry in the service of reform ideas would expand in the *Liberator* and other Bostonian magazines to cover a range of causes that included temperance, woman's suffrage, Native American rights, prison reform, educational reform, asylum reform, and so on. This rising culture of poetic didacticism would be mocked as "Frogpondian" croaking by Edgar Allan Poe in the 1840s and by Augustine Joseph Hickey Duganne (1823–84), whose 1850 satire *Parnassus in Pillory* takes aim at Boston's self-regard:

> No lead can fathom Boston's mental deep,
> No alien thought can scale her learning's steep:
> No fancy strains to that she does not reach,
> And none may learn save haply she shall teach.

In the first issue of the *Atlantic Monthly*, published in November 1857, its editor, James Russell Lowell (1819–91), who had written righteous antiwar and antislavery verse for years, was ready to surrender. In a poem called "The Origin of Didactic Poetry," he scorned the "pious plums" or truisms that informed much of Boston's literary output and advised poets to "put all your beauty in your rhymes, / Your morals in your living."

Though they deal with political matters, the poems chosen for this section predate the antebellum period with its controversial deployment of reform-advocacy verse. More exploratory and less predictable, these poems immerse us in political debates of the post-Revolutionary decades, a time when both specific events and social trends in Europe and the new United States provided grist for writers. Two poems that appeared on the same page of the March 1793 issue of the *Massachusetts Magazine* respond to issues and figures on different sides of the Atlantic. Depicting the recently reelected George Washington as a hero in both war and peace, "TO THE PRESIDENT. *Written on His arrival in* BOSTON" hails the most admired political figure of the 1790s. Events in France, including the then-recent execution of Louis XVI, provide material for the surprisingly sympathetic "STANZAS TO MARIA ANTONIETTA." Addressed to the then-imprisoned queen, the anonymous poet sees the French Revolution as a criminal undertaking and Antoinette as both a victim and a potential heroine:

> Daughter of woe! Maria! Queen!
> With calm composure meet the closing scene;
> Smile on the axe, the point of death defy,
> And let a woman teach a world to die.

A poem called "BUONAPARTE," published anonymously by Lydia Huntley Sigourney in the September 1816 issue of the *North American Review*, makes perhaps more familiar points about Napoleon. Appearing during Buonaparte's exile on Saint Helena, it sees him as a charismatic but monstrously immoral actor who deserves to spend the rest of his life in disgrace: "There let him sink, to teach them by his fate / The awful horrours of the guilty great."

"THE WAR HORSE," a revision of a text from Job that appeared in the September 1791 issue of the *Massachusetts Magazine*, removes the dramatic, biblical context, which has God asking Job a series of rhetorical questions designed to contrast God's power and knowledge with Job's comparative weakness and ignorance. Rather than serving as evidence of this theological point, the horse's frenzied, perhaps recklessly fearless, behavior in battle can be seen as a representation of the brutal and mindless passions stirred up by war. This is unambiguously the case for the more explicitly antiwar poems included here that appeared in the years

following the end of the War of 1812 in North America and the Napole-
onic wars abroad. Far more than the conventional celebration of peace
in a poem like *"Hymn, sung at Cambridge"* (*Christian Disciple*, March 3,
1815)—the inclusion of stanzas from English minister Joseph Fawcett's
radical, pre-Marxist poem "The Contrast" in the October 4, 1816, issue of
the *Christian Disciple* highlights the rise of pacifism in the city that gave
birth to the American Revolution. Appearing as "EXTRACTS FROM FAW-
CETT'S CONTRAST," the Boston text comprises only eleven of Fawcett's
original thirty-seven stanzas. Both versions invidiously compare an indi-
vidual murderer with those who use their control of state power to take
their countries to war:

> Ye who direct the social state,
> Which tauntingly ye civil call!
> Who whip the crimes yourselves create,
> Yourselves most criminal of all!

Nicholas A. Volpe, a member of our research team who studied both ver-
sions of this poem, notes that the original, longer text does much more
than the Bostonian revision to exculpate the individual killer. Cut from
the shorter text, five stanzas (20–25) in the original poem describe the
flawed nurture of the boy who grows up to commit murder, calling him
"society's deserted child" (stanza 20) and blaming "the great ones of the
globe" (stanza 25) for corrupting him. Their inculcation of bad values is
detailed in stanzas 22–24:

> Each rising scene of opening life
> To thy deluded fancy showed,
> For gold, one feverish, maddening strife,
> As gold contain'd all human good.
>
> The bloated sons of Luxury,
> With costly fare, to surfeit fed,
> Met, on each side, thine envious eye,
> And fired thy wish for more than bread.
>
> Thou saw'st Respect's uplifted eyes
> The rich, whate'er their crimes, adore,
> Thou saw'st the rich the poor despise,
> And thee despise for being poor.

Apparently unwilling to excuse any violence, Noah Worcester (1758–1837), the Bostonian editor and peace activist who revised and condensed Fawcett's poem, kept the focus on the "great ones of the globe" who, driven by greed, send soldiers to die in anguish on "fields of gore."

Approaching relations between people in different classes in a far lighter spirit, "NEW YEAR'S ADDRESS OF THE SWEEPERS" from the January 8, 1819, issue of the *New-England Galaxy and Masonic Magazine* pokes fun at other, seemingly superior professions by noting that they too sweep if only metaphorically:

> For cash, well your bodies the Doctor will sweep,
> The Lawyer, so knowing, cries, "Down with your dust;"
> And the Clergy—but hush, from the Order we'll keep,
> Or be sent to old Belzabub surely we must.

Other political positions that animate poems in this section include the universal benevolence and the embrace of all mankind in "The MAN of FEELING," which was reprinted in the November 1792 issue of the *Massachusetts Magazine* from a 1784 issue of *The Lady's Magazine* (London), and the opposite sentiment in a celebration of missionary work called "TRIBUTE TO FOREIGN MISSIONS," which appeared in the July 24, 1819, issue of the *Boston Recorder*. In the former, the speaker calls on Christians to join with Muslims and Jews in brotherhood. In the latter, the speaker celebrates New England pilgrims "who planted the banner of Christ on the shore, / and made the wild tribes disappear."

The rise of political parties in these decades generated poems of approval and discontent. The repudiation of partisan, sectarian politics rings out in both "EPIGRAM. When a Partizan dies of true Jacobin leaven" from the May 20, 1809, issue of the *Ordeal* and "Arduous the task in which we would engage" from the August 10, 1811, issue of the *Scourge*. The flip side of this debate, that is, rabidly partisan positions, can be found in "DEMOCRATS IN OFFICE" from the August 28, 1811, issue of the *Scourge* and "CANNING'S SPEECH" which ran in the *New-England Galaxy & Masonic Magazine* on October 31, 1817. Abolitionist sentiments drive "SPARE INJUR'D AFRICA! THE NEGRO SPARE!" from the August 29, 1818, issue of the *Boston Recorder*. Appealing for pity, the poet emphasizes the plight of slaves, declaring,

> No gentle home, replete with joys serene,
> Greets the poor negro friendless and forlorn;

Pensive he wanders o'er the world's rude scene,
The white man's laughter, & the white man's scorn.

Written from a wide range of political positions, the poems in this section suggest some of what passed through the minds of Bostonians as they perused these magazines for literary diversion and for news and commentary on current issues as well. The fact that the problems addressed in these poems—including slavery, contempt for others, partisan division, war, and inequality—still plague mankind creates what may be the most unfortunate links between the early national period and our own time.

The WAR HORSE.
From Job, xxxix Chap. 19th to 26th verse

See, the strong war steed, paw th' embattled vale,
    On his broad neck the vollied thunders roll;
His glowing nostrils scent the murky gale,
    And on he sweeps to glory's deathless goal.

Proud of great strength—he meets a host in arms,
    Mocks at pale fear—nor trembling turns away
From the drawn sword—unconscious of alarms,
    Not glittering spear—nor burnished shield affray.

Amid the rattling trump—Ha! ha! he cries;
Full sense of pleasure triumphs in his eyes;
For joy he disbelieves the clarion's sound;
The shouts increase, they catch his listening ear—
He spurns the bit, snuffs blood, nor stops to hear—
    But swallows, fierce with rage, the life-ensanguin'd ground.

Balbec, *Massachusetts Magazine*, October 1791

———

The MAN of FEELING.

THE wisest, weakest, have their woes,
I feel for all my suff'ring foes,
By anguish rack'd on ev'ry side,
In fierce affliction's furnace try'd:
We're brothers all by nature's laws,
Which bind not feelings to a cause,
But nobly urges to despise,
With minds expansive, local ties.

Can he, the christian, bring disgrace
On his own faith, when to the race
Who Mahomet's religion own,
His pity for their pangs is shone?
Relief each human creature claims,
Distrest—away with modes and names!
Jews, Turks, and Christians should unite,
To keep humanity in sight.

Each fine sensation of the breast,
Which gives to life its heightened zest,
From mutual aid proceeds—away,
Ye wretched of the coarser clay,
Whose cares are to yourselves confin'd,
Whose hearts ne'er throb for all mankind;
From them each sordid passion tear,
Which mean self love had planted there.

Anonymous, Massachusetts Magazine, November 1792

———

STANZAS TO MARIA ANTONIETTA.

DAUGHTER of woe! Maria! Queen!
For thus I hail thee 'mid a scene,
Where Liberty exchang'd for crime,
Has dipt in gore the robe of time.

Madd'ning I see the raging fiend,
  Who rides on desolation's flood,
  Bathe his red arm in human blood,
And leave you widow'd of a friend.

Thy *Lamballe*[†] falls—thy *Louis* dies;
  The dauphin gluts the insatiate grave;
And fell barbarity with ruthless cries,
  Demands thy head, the victim of the glaive.[†]

Daughter of woe! Maria! Queen!
With calm composure meet the closing scene;
Smile on the axe, the point of death defy,
And let a woman teach the world to die.

AURELIA, Massachusetts Magazine, March 1793

[†]*Lamballe*: Princess Maria Teresa of Savoy-Carignan (1749–92), Marie Antoinette's friend who was brutally executed in September of 1792; *glaive*: a sword or lance.

TO THE PRESIDENT.
Written on his arrival at BOSTON.

ILLUSTRIOUS patriot, hero, sage,
Ordain'd to save a future age,
 Before *Columbia's* birth:
The father, friend of human kind,
To whom the Almighty Sire consign'd
 His noblest charge on earth:

Grand base of freedom's fed'rate dome,
More glorious far than *Greece* or *Rome*,
 In noon's meridian glow;
The pride of battle's crimson'd plain;
The hope of concord's raptur'd train;
 The sun of peace below:

If whilst loud peans rend the sky,
And tears of transport fill each eye,
 The muse could claim thine ear;
Her voice should swell the choreal song,
Which grateful thousands shout along,
 In lays sublime, sincere.

But not the poet's boldest strain,
The patriot's lyre, nor hero train,
 Can eternize such worth:
To seraph forms that task is giv'n;
And trumpet tongues of elder heav'n,
 Forbid the praise of earth.

D., Massachusetts Magazine, March 1793

THE DYING INDIAN.

WORN with fatigue, oppress'd with age at last,
Pining with pain brave *Altamaha*[†] lies,
Around on all his anxious eyes are cast,
And draw attention while he speaks and dies.

My friends ye are welcome on my dying day;
I'm pleas'd to see you thus attend your chief;
If ought on earth could chase my pain away,
Your kind attention sure would bring relief.

I've trod life's journey with a steady pace,
Your friends I've cherish'd and your foes I've fought
Nor *Altamaha* e'er deny'd his face,
To hapless mortal who his friendship sought.

The lonely stranger if to us he came,
Found here a safe retreat from all his foes;
We wav'd inquiry of his rank or name,
And spread the furry skin for his repose.

I weep, but oh my friends the cause is great,
That wrings these tears from Altamaha's eyes;
I leave you when I fear impending fate,
With angry frowns will bid new sorrows rise.

Soon, soon a ghost I feel your chief must be,
Which wounds my spirit, pains my doubting mind;
Fain would I pierce the unknown shades to see,
The state and fortunes of our wretched kind!

But hush my tongue, nor mention private woes,
Fond self intrude not at this painful hour;
For lo, the *whites* as old tradition goes,
Contract our limits, and destroy our power.

And the *Great Spirit* still neglects our woes,
And arms with vengeance those we kindly fed;
Nay, lends his thunder to our artful foes,
Whose blast terrific, strikes the warrior dead.

Ah, dreadful thoughts still stealing on my soul,
Paint future days which urge me to despair;
When you my sons shall wander to the pole,
To seek from christian vengeance, refuge there.

Yes you must quit the land your fathers gave,
Must yield the mountain and the peaceful vale;
Or basely lose the man — commence the slave,
And vent your sighs with ev'ry passing gale.

When last these eyes by weariness were closed,
Me-thought my spirit sought the shades to know:
But thron'd in darkness, demons interpos'd,
And frown'd indignant on your chief below.

Successive thunders then around me roll'd,
And strong convulsions shook the dismal wood;
But still unshaken, firm, and uncontrol'd
Incas'd in darkness, Altamaha stood.

While yet their horrors, echoing struck mine ears,
A voice more dreadful swept the dark'ned plain,
Whose accents planted in my breast those fears
Which I've related in prophetic strain.

"Forbear, rash chief, t'attempt the shades below,"
(In thund'ring voice the angry demon said,)
"Nor strive the deep designs of fate to know,
Lest woes immortal rest upon thine head!"

"Yet know, fond chief, thy nation's doom'd a prey,
To those they fed and kindly did embrace!
The time's not distant when the spreading day,
Shall scarce illume a son of all thy race."

The demon then with kindly step withdrew,
Lock'd up his thunder and roll'd back the storm:
My native country then advanc'd to view,
But oh, how alter'd from its present form!

The cruel *whites* with fierce vindictive ire,
Persuade our tribes, obliged by fate to fly;
The forest gleam'd with unrelenting fire,
And flames destructive light the northern sky.

O'er the plain sad desolation spread,
And riffled[†] nature wore a gloomy face;
Each useful tenant of the land had fled,
With all the blessings that attend the chase.

Such were the scenes that struck my mental eyes,
While sunk insensate in the arms of sleep;
And 'tis for this that Altamaha sighs,
And lost in anguish stoops for once to weep.

But fly, my sons, to earth's remotest bounds,
New forests seek where rolls an unknown sky;
To other worlds, if other can be found,
Retire as free or here as freemen die.

The Indian's God, methinks may yet arise,
Reclaim for us, our lost, our native rights;
And fortune, changeful as the varying skies,
May frown at last upon the cruel *whites*.

But now no more I meet your daring foes,
No more the stranger shares my doubtful bread;
To lands unknown your chief reluctant goes,
And sinks forgotten with the sleeping dead."

Thus spake the chief with tear-devoted eye,
To weeping friends, involv'd in deepest woe;
Then drew a long—a sad distressing sigh,
And sunk lamented to the shades below.

ZAMA, *Boston Weekly Magazine*, March 26, 1803

[†]*Altamaha*: seventeenth-century Native American (Yamasee) chief; *riffled*: damaged by wind or storm

————

EPIGRAM. [In the reign of Democracy, dead to all shame]

In the reign of Democracy, dead to all shame,
The demons of falsehood infest us;
Vice and Folly assume Wit and Virtue's fair name,
And the devil himself's call'd *Honestus*.

Anonymous, *The Ordeal*, May 13, 1809

EPIGRAM. [When a Partizan dies of true Jacobin leaven]

When a Partizan dies of true Jacobin leaven,
Where he'll go 'tis not easy to tell;
For a king he must have, if he goes up to heaven,
And a king if he goes down to hell.

Anonymous, Ordeal, May 20, 1809

———

[Arduous the task in which we would engage]

Arduous the task in which we would engage—
To lash the numerous follies of the age:
To watch the machinations of that band,
Who aim to spread destruction through the land;
To expose the insidious knave; and mark the crimes,
Which float upon the current of the times;
To hurl the slaves of faction from the stage,
And on them pour an incens'd people's rage;
To wrest from ignorant hands the reins of power;
To tell Democracy her day is o'er;
To speak of times that *were*—and, with a tear,
T'dvert[†] to melancholy days that *are*;
In short, to extend the beneficial sway
Of *Federal virtue* in the present day.

Anonymous [the editor?], Scourge, August 10, 1811

[†]*T'dvert*: to advert, that is, to call attention.

———

DEMOCRATS IN OFFICE.

In times of general agitation,
Some rise like scum in fermentation;
Who push and kick the whole world up-
Side down, to get themselves a-top;
And when they've gain'd their fav'rite point,
For want of strength can't move a joint;
As useless as a leaky cask,
Or like a furnace out of blast;

Who shortly must be laid aside,
Like horse, unfit to draw or ride.

Anonymous, *Scourge*, August 28, 1811

————

Hymn, sung at Cambridge, at the celebration of peace.

Almighty God! to Thee we bow,
To Thee the voice of gladness raise;
Thy mercy, that hath blessed us now,
In loud and grateful songs we praise.
Long hast thou stretched the avenging hand,
And smote thy people in thy wrath;
Hast frowned upon a guilty land,
While storms and darkness veiled thy path.

But light from heaven has shone at last,
And PEACE is beaming from above,
The storm of doubt and fear has past,
And hope returns, and joy, and love.
Then praise to that Eternal Power,
Who bids our wars and tumults cease,
And hymn, in this auspicious hour,
The God of Mercy—God of Peace.

Anonymous, *Christian Disciple*, March 3, 1815

————

LINES COMPOSED ON HEARING THE NEWS OF PEACE

WHAT joyful sounds are those, that greet mine ear?
The pleasing news of PEACE, once more I hear!
Heaven looks serene, the stars more brilliant shine,
And smiling nature wears a look divine.
The dreadful sound of WAR is heard no more,
The trumpet's blast, nor thundering cannon roar;
But dove-like Peace her blooming olive bears,
She bids us smile, and dissipate our fears.
Husbands again, their faithful wives shall greet,
And tender parents, and their children meet—
Brothers and sisters, shall again embrace,

And joy and gladness animate each face.
Let hymns of praise and gratitude arise,
To that great GOD, who rules both earth and skies,
May peace and love, and liberty abound,
And pure religion in our hearts be found.
Then may we hope to reach that happy shore,
When sighs and sorrow shall be known no more;
Where all the region breathes eternal peace,
And where our songs of praise shall never cease.
Andover, February 15, 1815.

Julia, Christian Disciple, January 4, 1816

———————

*There appeared in the newspapers some months since, a character of
Buonaparte, drawn with energy and truth; most of the ideas and expressions
of it will be found in the following lines, which are offered for the North-
American Review.*

BUONAPARTE.

The drama sinks, the tragick scene is o'er,
And he who mov'd the springs is seen no more:
He, whose mad course was still to Virtue blind,
Whose stage the world, whose auditors mankind,
Whose plot unfolding, fill'd the earth with tears
Now lost, disgrac'd, abandon'd, disappears.
When first, with eagle eye and vulture's rage,
He rush'd in strides of fury o'er the stage,
He rais'd the curtain with his dagger's blade,
And pour'd red carnage o'er the slumbering shade.
His dreadful part, terrifick, strange and new,
Nor fancy follow'd, nor Experience drew,
It sprang inventive from a daring mind,
Where malice, nerve, and intellect combin'd.
Nurs'd by ambition, for a moment slept
In a stern heart where feeling never wept,
Thence bursting rapid, changeless in its aim,
Gave birth to deeds that language cannot name.
With battle clouds the shrinking sun he veil'd,
With wasting fires the startled night assail'd,

Mark'd on the ravag'd earth his dire pursuit,
By her torn blossoms, and her wither'd fruit;
Without a signal, to the field he rush'd,
O'er friends enslav'd, and faithful allies crush'd:
High from the Alps, amid eternal snow,
He pour'd his legions on the vale below;
In desolation's tone his armour rang,
War follow'd war, from conquest, conquest sprang;
He fought in Scythia's caves, on Africk's sands,
Chas'd the wild Arab mid his roving bands,
Perch'd on the pyramids, in dizzy height,
Look'd down with scorn on Alexander's might;
O'er Europe's realm like Attila he rush'd,
He snatch'd, divided, subjugated, crush'd,
Here, planted minions in his smile to reign,
There, captive monarchs groan'd beneath his chain.
The Roman pontiff trembled at his rod,
Which proudly prest the altar of his God,
While Albion's fleets, whose sides with lightning glow,
Were seen like Argus,[†] watching for their foe,
And her white cliffs, in close array were lin'd,
With anxious soldiers on their arms reclin'd:
For, like the blasting Siroch's[†] baleful breath,
His path was strew'd with misery and death.
As on the flashing meteor, bright and dread,
Each eye was fix'd, where'er his madness led:
And if his pride exulted in the fame,
What heart could wonder, or what voice could blame?
Could mortal eye endure, with steady sight,
The dazzling pomp of such tremendous height?
Who, that unhurt, and undismay'd had stood
Mid slaughter'd myriads in the fields of blood,
But would suppose his temper'd armour given
Like stern Achilles, from the forge of heaven?
—Admiring awe beheld his glories tow'r,
And France forgot her chains to share his pow'r,
E'en the pale conscript left without a sigh,
Home, love, and liberty, for him to die.
Proud Genius, bending, strew'd her venal lays;
The servile arts were listed in his praise,

While blood stain'd victory, in trophies bore,
The ravish'd spoils of rich Italia's shore.
—In that proud city, where his arching throne
On ruin rais'd, with sudden brilliance shone,
Time laid aside his scythe, to gaze with joy
And linger among charms he never could destroy.
—While the old world, to meet its offspring came,
Sages and chiefs who join'd the march of fame,
Claim with delighted eye and tone sublime,
A milder sentence on the tyrant's crime.
—But how can Europe grant the kind appeal?
Reft† of her sons, and wounded by his steel!
Where is a couch so dark, a cell so deep
That burning Moscow's memory there should sleep?
What, can the scenes of purple Jaffa blot?
And when shall Loda's slaughter be forgot?
Who from a future age shall hide the view
Of Jena, Austerlitz, and Waterloo?
Earth clad in sable, never can forego
The deepen'd trace, or man forget the wo.
Yet let him live, if life can yet be born
Disrob'd of glory, and deprest with scorn;
Yes, let him live! if he to life can bend
Without a follower, and without a friend:
If from the hand he hated, he can bear
To take the gift, his stain'd existence spare,
Who from his lonely island shall exclude
The fearful step of Conscience foul with blood?
What cuirass† guard his breast with temper'd force
From the keen shaft of pitiless remorse?
Oh! in his awful cell of guilt and fear
Stretch the red map that marks his dire career,
Light the funeral torch, in ruin spread
His reeking hecatombs† of mangled dead,
And if to hearts like his Contrition comes,
There let him seek her mid impending glooms;
There let him live, and to mankind display
The mighty miseries of ambition's sway;
There let him sink, to teach them by his fate
The awful horrours of the guilty great.

Great, in the stores of a malignant mind;
Great, in the deeds that desolate mankind;
Great, like the pestilence in sable shroud,
That darts its arrow from the midnight cloud;
Great, like the whirlwind in its wrecking path,
To sow in evil, and to reap in wrath.

Anonymous [Lydia Huntley Sigourney], *North American Review*, September 1816

[†]*Argus*: Argus Panotes, one-hundred-eyed and, thus, ever-watchful giant in Greek my-
thology; *Siroch* (Sirocco): the hot wind that blows from North Africa across the Mediter-
ranean Sea; *Reft*: bereft; *cuirass*: defensive armor that protects the torso, front, and back;
hecatomb: the sacrifice or killing of numerous victims.

———

EXTRACTS FROM FAWCETT'S CONTRAST.

DARK dismal pictures now employ
My pensive breast, and thence expel
All lightsome forms of gentle joy;
Ye smiling images, farewell!

Dire scenes succeed. The tragick blade
Gleams horrible thro' night's dun gloom!
And Murder, shrouded in the shade,
Steals soft along th' invaded room!

Reveal'd by morn, the midnight deed
Suspends the pale discoverer's breath!
I hear the scream of horrour spread!
I see the purple couch of death!

The murderer flies; but flies in vain;
Seized by the out-stretch'd arm of law;
The sullen prisoner clanks his chain,
Laid hopeless on the scatter'd straw.

Oh, iron state of rude mankind,
'T'hou[†] human thing, of man accurst,
What virtues would have warm'd thy mind,
Had scenes of kindlier influence nurst.

Thou saw'st the great ones of the globe,
To their too much yet adding more,
Array'd in robes of honour, rob
And deluge fields with seas of gore.

Thou know'st that on their blood-stain'd plain,
In dying anguish millions groan!
And, thy more humble ends to gain,
Thine arm was rais'd to murder *one*.

Then they, whose ill tuition sow'd
(Too quick of growth) the baneful seed,
The plant with fierce intolerance mow'd,
Because it proved a noxious weed.

Ye who direct the social state,
Which tauntingly ye civil call!
Who whip the crimes yourselves create,
Yourselves most criminal of all!

Cannot the city's ample room,
Your polity's dark frowns confine,
That thus they speed their angry gloom.
Where loveliest nature smiles benign?

Instructed in this genial school,
Mellow your crude, inclement plan,
Copy mild Nature's gentle rule,
And learn, like her, to smile on man!

Joseph Fawcett, *Christian Disciple*, October 4, 1816

†*Thou*: there are at least three possible antecedents for this ambiguous pronoun: (1) the state as government, (2) the human condition as illustrated in the plight of the specific murderer who is addressed directly in the rest of the stanza and in the next two stanzas; (3) the murderer.

CANNING'S SPEECH.

Enigma.
Come tell me, if it is not past thy reach—
Why is a beggar like George Canning's Speech?[†]

Solution
The simile is most complete if we grant—
For Canning's speech is nothing but VAGueRANT.

Anonymous, New-England Galaxy and Masonic Magazine, October 31, 1817

[†]*George Canning*: (1770–1827), British politician and statesman.

EPITAPH on a Tomb-Stone
found in the graveyard in Concord, upon a Negro-Slave, who by his constant labor during the hours which he could steal from his daily tasks, was enabled to purchase his freedom.

God wills us free;
Man wills us slaves;
I will as God wills;
God's will be done.
Here lies the body of John Jack,
A native of Africa, who died April A.D. 1773
Aged about sixty years.
Tho' born in a land of slaves,
He was born free.
Tho' he lived in a land of liberty,
He lived a slave.
Till by his honest, though stolen labors
He acquired the source of slavery,
Which gave him his freedom,
Tho' not long before
Death the grand *Tyrant*,
Gave him his final *emancipation*.
And set him on a footing with Kings.
Tho' a slave to vice,
He practiced those virtues,
Without which *Kings* are but *slaves*.

Anonymous, Boston Recorder, July 7, 1818

"SPARE INJUR'D AFRICA! THE NEGRO SPARE!"

Lives there a wretch array'd in human form,
Whose iron heart no soft affection knows,
Who treats the cause of Africa with scorn,
Nor drops one tear of pity for her woes.

O injur'd country! doom'd to be unblest,
The galling yoke of slavery doom'd to wear,
Thy wretched souls in foreign lands opprest,
To heaven for vengeance raise the ceaseless pray'r.

And shall the ceaseless prayer be rais'd in vain?
O will not heaven in anger lift the rod,
And crush the wretch who dares for sordid gain,
To buy, to sell, to mar the works of God?

Detested traffic! base, inhuman, vile,
Which barters human flesh and human bones,
Which dooms to misery, slavery and exile,
Poor helpless thousands born to sighs and groans.

Tho' liberty, sweet sound! may reach their ears,
Yet are their woes e'en then but half redrest,
Worn out with toils, they spend the tedious years
Far from that country where their fathers rest.

No gentle home, replete with joys serene,
Greets the poor negro friendless and forlorn;
Pensive he wanders o'er the world's rude scene,
The white man's laughter, & the white man's scorn.

Veronica, *Boston Recorder*, August 29, 1818

NEW YEAR'S ADDRESS OF THE SWEEPERS

Mr. Editor, The following was written at the particular request of a
learned Librarian of the town; and was meant for the use of Mr. Handy,
or some other of his profession. By some accident, it did not appear
among the Addresses of last New-Year's Day. I wrote it; and, believing
it to be an excellent production, send it to you as a particular favor, for
publication in the Galaxy.

Ye gentlemen gay, who so proud of your shoes,
    And so fearful of dust, wish the town from dust clear;
Give the Sweeper a ninepence, or more, if you choose,
    In return for his wishing you happy new-year.

Despise not his calling—there's many a wight
    That sweeps in vast style, tho' we see not the broom;
And there's many a Dandy, from morning to night
    That kicks up a dust in some street or ballroom.

Look on 'Change, and just mark how the rhino[†] is swept
    Into pockets of brokers, and shavers, and banks;
And at Barrister's Hall, too, a besom[†] is kept
    For brushing up rogues in their delicate pranks.

For cash, well your bodies the Doctor will sweep,
    The Lawyer, so knowing, cries, "Down with your dust;"
And the Clergy—but hush, from the Order we'll keep,
    Or be sent to old Belzabub surely we must.

All are sweepers in *some way*, if not in the street,
    And he's the most cunning and laudable elf;
Who cares not a farthing for passengers neat,
    So he sees his way clear—and from dirt keep *himself.*

P. P., *New-England Galaxy and Masonic Magazine*, January 8, 1819

[†]*rhino*: slang term for money; *besom*: a broom usually made with twigs.

TRIBUTE TO FOREIGN MISSIONS.
Written by a stranger in Boston, in June, 1819.

How blest is the land where the pilgrims repose,
    Whose faith could their sorrows beguile;
Who bid this peninsula bloom as the rose,
    Who bid the late wilderness smile.

With rapture I gaze on the ocean that bore,
    My Christianiz'd ancestors here;
Who planted the banner of Christ on the shore,
    And made the wild tribes disappear.

Now back to the east towards Bethlehem's star,
    Religion makes light to arise;
Her reign breathes destruction to Juggernaut's car,
    Before her idolatry dies.

Ye winds and ye waves, O propitiously move,
    To waft the glad tidings of peace,
Till all men are brought to repentance and love,
    Till warfare and wickedness cease.

Thrice happy ye Christians, whose bosoms still glow,
    With piety's noblest design;
Your land is exempted from war and from woe,
    And grace gives you blessings divine.

In loveliness, charity beams o'er the waves,
    And blesses the earth with her smiles;
She sends to all countries the gospel that saves,
    And offers her gifts to the isles.

O Thou who dos't walk on the wings of the wind,
    And rule the tempestuous sea,
Speak peace to the ocean, give light to the blind,
    That missions may glorify thee.

O bless and protect all thy children of light
　　Who sail to a far distant shore;
O guide and protect them in life by thy might,
　　Till life and its cares are no more.

B.G., *Boston Recorder*, July 24, 1819

————

SLAVE-HOLDER AND YANKEE

A Yankee wag once took a range
To southern states, where all seem'd strange;
For every white one had a black
Toiling and sweating at his back;
Each had a slave, in dinner room,
To give assistance and perfume.

Our Yankee knew not to behave
With etiquette toward a slave,
So watch'd, as cat would watch a mouse,
The conduct of the man o' th' house.

"Here, John," says he, "carve me a slice
Of meat, that's delicate and nice.
Now take it and with caution lay't
And cut it fine upon my plate."
This done, the Buckskin took his fork,
And quickly set his jaws to work.

The Yankee being fond of fun,
Determin'd not to be outdone:
So the same orders issued strait,
Till meat was cut upon his plate;
Then to black Tom he smartly halloos,
Commanding him to do as follows;
"Now put it in my mouth—quick do it—
Now work my jaws, while I shall chew it."

Anonymous, *Ladies' Port Folio*, April 29, 1820

THE FAMILY

Residence of Jeffrey Richardson, corner of High and Pearl Streets, Boston, erected 1794. Courtesy of the Bostonian Society

Two books written at the start of the American Studies movement in the early 1980s—Jay Fliegelman's *Prodigals and Pilgrims: The American Revolution against Patriarchal Authority, 1750–1800*, and Kathy N. Davidson's *Revolution and the Word: The Rise of the Novel in America*—provide useful frames for reading the poems about family relations collected here. Fliegelman follows the transition in both England and America that began in the middle of the eighteenth century:

> An older patriarchal family authority was giving way to a new parental ideal characterized by a more affectionate and equalitarian relationship with children. This important development paralleled the emergence of a humane form of childrearing that accommodated the stages of a child's growth and recognized the distinctive character of childhood. Parents who embraced the new childrearing felt a deep moral commitment to prepare their children for a life of rational independence and moral self-sufficiency.

Davidson reads the early American novel, which first appeared in the 1790s, as a "political and cultural forum" in which ideas about gender relations were explored. Both conservative and progressive novelists responded to the underlying inequality of family relations: "Although the situation varied from state to state, . . . before marriage a young woman was typically considered the property of her father. . . . Marriage, for the women involved, was mostly a change in masters." Not only in fiction but across the discourse of the early national period, ideas about how to be a good parent, spouse, and sibling were addressed and debated, in both earnest and comic modes.[1]

The case for affectionate parenting and against harsh discipline animates the first poem in this section, Judith Sargent Murray's epigraph for a 1790 essay "On the Domestic Education of Children." Arguing against severe punishment inflicted by "unmanly," "tyrannical" authority figures, Murray calls for "mildness" and pointedly asks, "What can an infant do to merit blows?" Affection between generations runs through several of the other works in this section. Murray's birthday invitation—("JULIA, to ANNA MARIA, sends greeting") in the November 20, 1802, issue of the *Boston Weekly Magazine*—is a veritable bouquet of floral decoration that honors the love between two infant cousins, while Susanna Rowson's "Thanksgiving," published in the next issue of the same magazine, places religious gratitude and support for charity in a domestic scene of "sportive love and sacred friendship." An affirmation of parental care also underpins the heartfelt appeal for the adoption of an orphan in a poem from the May 8, 1819, issue of the *Boston Recorder*—just as longing for domestic comfort informs "To the American Goldfinch" from the June 14, 1817, issue of the *Boston Weekly Magazine*.

"A GRANDMOTHER, TO HER INFANT GRANDCHILD"—which appeared in the April 1, 1820, issue of the *Ladies' Port Folio*—showcases intergenerational criticism of a negligent father. The four stanzas of "A MOTHER's LOVE" in the November 11, 1820, issue of the *Christian Watchman* were extracted from the original ten-stanza poem by James Montgomery, British editor and poet, which was published in London in 1819. The condensed version, like the original, celebrates the sweetness and warmth of watching, breastfeeding, and guiding a "helpless babe": "To smile and listen when it talks, / And lend a finger when it walks; / This is a Mother's Love." It is interesting to note, however, that the Boston extract omits the dark turn Montgomery takes in the longer version when he asks, "Can a mother's love grow cold?" and insists that "the infant reared alone for earth, / May live, may die—to curse his birth." By cutting lines that denounce secular mothering, the editor reflects the rise of universalism and Unitarianism in Boston.

In other poems here, strife between parents and children and between husbands and wives is central. The comic lament "LINES *Written by an old Planter, in the country, to his daughter*," from the March 1800 issue of the *Columbian Phenix and Boston Review*, criticizes a young woman who squandered money on clothing and jewelry during her trip to the city. The contrast between the "frugal, neat, and plain" style in which she left home and the decked-out "Holland Doll" she becomes is amusing, as is the anxiety her dad expresses at the end:

> These muslins, satins, muslinet,
> God knows, have brought a serious debt;
> . . . You may indulge your modish tricks,
> But I'm no fool at fifty-six.

Because he is exasperated, the father provides a hilariously detailed litany of then-current fashion trends on display at dry goods stores, including silks, lawn, foreign gewgaws, "India shawls of camel's hair," "silver'd shoes, and color'd veils." Readers today will feel a shock of recognition when he mocks her "pound-weight" earrings and prophetically protests, "As well might vanities like those / Be seen suspended from your nose."

A more serious account of father-daughter relations appears in "ELIZA . . . *A Poem*," from the April 1810 issue of *Something*, in which the daughter of a Revolutionary War veteran is seduced and ruined by an immoral soldier. Driven to madness by reckless decisions, Eliza bids

> Farewell to duty—farewell every thought
> That virtue sanction'd, confidence inspir'd;
> Maternal fondness now no more was sought,
> Her father's virtues now no more inspir'd.

If "ELIZA . . . *A Poem*" promotes filial piety through a story of harmful disobedience, "JEPHTHAH'S VOW" (*Christian Watchman*, December 1811) uses a seemingly opposite narrative to enforce the same social norm. The poem adds emotional depth to the Old Testament story about an unwise Israelite leader who kills his daughter after promising to sacrifice "the first being" he sees when he gets home from combat. Unlike naughty Eliza, Jephthah's unnamed, doomed daughter quickly accepts her undeserved destiny, moving from "a wild cry of despair" to acceptance and prayers for her father's well-being:

> "O comfort him, Heaven, when low in the dust
> My limbs are inactively laid!
> O comfort him, Heaven, and let him then trust,
> That free and immortal the souls of the just
> Are in glory and beauty arrayed."

Alexandra Mitropoulos, a member of our research team who studied this poem, notes that Jephthah's six-year rule took place in a long line of Israelite kings who did evil in the sight of the Lord, and that his vow (as described in Judges 11:31) should, therefore, be seen as reckless, even terrible. Unlike Abraham, who complies with the Lord's instruction and is prevented from killing his son at the last moment, Jephthah acts on his own initiative. "JEPHTHAH'S VOW" reframes the story, leaving out details of the war and focusing on the emotional responses of everyone involved. Heartbroken, Jephthah moves through alarm and horror to lifelong grief. After a moment of frenzy, the daughter embraces her bereft father, rushing to his arms, "and there as a flower when chill'd by the blast, / Reclines on an oak while its fury may last, / On his bosom she hush'd her alarms." While onlookers' eyes are "moistened in woe," "religion's sweet self" allows the daughter to behave in a saintly manner. The tear-stained lines of this poem remind us of both the rising role of sentimentality and the enduring importance of biblical texts in moral teaching about family relations during the early national period.

Shifting from the sentimental to the gothic, "LORD DYRING . . . A BALLAD," from the October 6, 1810, issue of the *Harvard Lyceum*, is a ghost story about a mother who returns from the dead to protect her children from their cruel stepmother and negligent father. The mother's reunion with her younger children is touching in a macabre way:

> She came to the tower where the babes did lie,
> She kissed away every tear;
> To the eldest daughter she says, "now hie,
> And send Lord Dyring here."
>
> She dressed up *this* with a mother's care,
> Another she brushed so clean,
> Like a mother she combed the third one's hair,
> And folded his ruffle so sheen.

Trouble between spouses flares in poems like "THE RETROSPECT; *or*—ALL FOR THE BEST," from the January 22, 1806, issue of the *Fly*, and "The Consolation," that was reprinted from earlier publication in London in the April 12, 1812, issue of the *Boston Satirist*. In the former, the speaker suffers so much from his wife's "mauling" that he contemplates suicide and rejoices when she dies instead; in the latter, a husband is reconciled to the fact that his house burned down by the comforting thought that his wife died in the fire! More conventional concerns appear in "The Effects of Intemperance" from the *Christian Disciple* in March of 1814. In it, a talented, learned, kind, and virtuous husband and father destroys himself and his family by drinking:

> To drown his cares, he drinks the more,
> And hurries on with staggering pace;
> He sinks in death, and leaves the world
> O'erwhelmed in guilt, despair, disgrace!

Family also serves as the setting for broader political and social concerns in "*Stanzas Addressed by a Lady in Vermont to her brother in the army*" from the January 8, 1820, issue of the *Ladies' Port Folio*, in which the speaker thinks about her brother away at war. At first she feels "patriotic zeal" and welcomes "the battle from afar." Later, fainting and aghast, she imagines the "crimson gore" of battle and her "brother's corpse."

While the works in this section only begin to represent the ways in which family relations evolved in these decades, they provide lively encounters with changing social norms and specific family members. By inviting us to attend parties, sit by firesides, visit gravesites, and overhear expressions of affection, disapproval, hostility, fear, and love, they draw us into the most intimate circles of Boston's social life.

NOTE

1. Jay Fliegelman, *Prodigals and Pilgrims: The American Revolution against Patriarchal Authority, 1750–1800* (Cambridge, MA: Cambridge University Press, 1982), 1–2; Kathy N. Davidson, *Revolution and the Word: The Rise of the Novel in America* (New York: Oxford University Press, 1986), 118.

On the DOMESTIC EDUCATION of CHILDREN

I hate severity to trembling youth,
Mildness should designate each useful truth;
My soul detests the rude unmanly part,
Which swells with bursting sighs the little heart.
What can an infant do to merit blows?
See, from his eyes a briny torrent flows.
Behold the pretty mourner! pale his cheek,
His tears are fruitless, and he dare not speak.
Lowly he bends beneath yon tyrant's rod;
Unfeeling pedagogue—who like some god
Fabled of old, of bloody savage mind,
To scourge, and not to mend the human race, design'd.

Constantia [Judith Sargent Murray], *Massachusetts Magazine*, May 1790

———

VERSES ON A SLEEPING DAUGHTER

MUCH lov'd infant, lull'd to rest,
By a mother's blessings blest;
Be thy slumbers soft and mild,
Sleep of cares and pain beguil'd;
Till the rising rosy morn,
Sowing pearls shall earth adorn;
Then amid parental bow'rs,
Sportive, playful pass thy hours;
Whilst a mother's constant care,
Shields, protects her darling fair.

Ah! this bosom how it beats!
Lo, the circling moment fleets;
Rapid flies the passing hour,
Leading on to hymen's bow'r;
Care and pains will then intrude,
These the portion of the good,
Virtue's self is frequent try'd,
Sleep and rest are oft deni'd;
Wakeful nights, and toilsome days;
Vex, confuse, disturb, amaze;

Pleasures fly, and cares and pain,
Then commence their tort'ring reign.

Sephoronia, Massachusetts Magazine, January 1793

———

LINES *written by an old Planter, in the country,*
to his daughter, who having gone in her plain country
dress to reside in the city, returned after some months
tricked off in all the gaudy attire of the gay world.

HOW, PHEBE, can I else but snarl,
When you, who went a country girl,
In habit frugal, neat and plain,
That might attract some rural swain;
Who never dreamt of silk or lawn,
Nor rov'd beyond our county town;
I say, how could you thus return
A Holland Doll?—Who did adorn
Your head in this prodigious dress,
Of foreign gewgaws, and not less
Than live-oak tops on yonder bluff,
A mountain of fantastic stuff?
Now, by flirtation's self, I swear,
You must your old apparel wear;
Those glitt'ring follies lay aside,
That feed at once your sloth and pride,
Put on again your home-spun geer,
And drop those pound-weights from your ear;
As well might vanities like those
Be seen suspended from your nose.
You shall not wear Morocco caps—
For idle beaus they may be traps;
But, though acquired at high expense,
Will never catch a man of sense.
What fops will now besiege my door
Attracted by that Dry Goods Store,
In every form which cut and hack'd,
Is to your idle carcass tack'd;

But let them fear the vengeance due
To all I catch in quest of you;
Of such gay birds you may be vain,
But mind—I tell you—*there's my cane.*
Far hence from us be China's ware,
Or India shawls of camel's hair;
These quiltings, quilted at Marseilles,
And silver'd shoes, and color'd veils;
I execrate all trash like that,
Nor shall you wear Suwarrow's* hat.
These muslins, satins, muslinet,
God knows, have brought a serious debt;
You PHEBE, do not count the cost
Of time mis-spent and labour lost;
You may indulge your modish tricks,
But I'm no fool at fifty-six;
These ribbands, edgings and gallons,
Will make me sing some dismal tunes,
Will force me when the *bill* is read,
To bite my nails and scratch my head,
If PHEBE does not for me feel,
And turn again the spinning-wheel.

Anonymous, Columbian Phenix and Boston Review, March 1800

Suwarrow: an atoll in the Cook Islands [original note].

———

[JULIA, to ANNA MARIA, sends greeting]

MESSERS. EDITORS, *As you have inserted my Cradle Piece so handsomely, I follow it by a* BIRTH-DAY INVITATION, written some months after, which if you give with equal accuracy, you shall hear again from a sincere well wisher to your very laudable undertaking. HONORA MARTESIA.

JULIA, to ANNA MARIA,[†] sends greeting,
For though but a youngling, she aims to be prating;
And now having rounded completely a year,
She wishes to make her importance appear.

She would, if she could, pen the love speaking lay,
To ANNA MARIA impressively say,
Come hither sweet girl—for it is the return
Of the annual day on which I was born;
Come hither, with me commencing the year,
The first in my circle of friends to appear.

Come see how Mamma, the best flowers culling,
Each vase and each pot this morn hath been filling,
With foilage so verdant adorning the room,
The air by their various sweets to perfume.

Here the holly-hock stands so gracefully tall,
And the nasturtion creeps over the wall;
The globe amaranthine—perpetual flower,
Arranged in pots fresh beauties discover;
The garden is ransack'd, and all to disclose,
The gladness supreme in her bosom which flows;
Come see the best flowerets how she hath twin'd,
A wreath for the brow of her daughter design'd;
Where the purple so rich conspicuous blooms,
And every leaf added beauty assumes;
A wreath which for fragrance and colour might vie,
With the rose of Salency,† or hue of the sky,
And which is intended my temples to crown,
On the very same hour which made me her own.
Come receive, my sweet girl, the charming bouquet,
Made up by her hand as a present for thee;
Where gillies, and lark-spurs, and pinks not a few,
Are shaded and grac'd by the marvel peru;
Where jessamines mingling with each pretty blow,
Are combined, her love and her fancy to show.

Of the ham and the chickens, too she would tell,
The pudding and custards in which we excel;
The tea and the cakes, bread and butter and cream,
That nothing imperfect nor wanting may seem;
While garlands of flowers shall garnish each dish,
As many as ANNA MARIA can wish.*

And gradually passing from each grosser scene,
To paint a futurity gaily serene;
When ANNA and JULIA in friendship's soft bands,
Their *hearts* shall immingle, uniting their hands,
When Amity genial shall open to them,
Esteem the rich fruit, and sweet kindred the stem;
This good still unfading kind heaven will give,
If well *we* design, and discreetly we live.

'Tis thus, if she could, the Gipsey would chatter,
But she is but a child, and so 'tis no matter;
While wanting the power we only can say,
Come, ANNA MARIA, and spend the white-day.

Honora Martesia [Judith Sargent Murray], *Boston Weekly Magazine*, November 20, 1802

*ANNA MARIA can wish: The beautiful little girl, since deceased, to which the invitation was addressed, early evinced the delicacy of her intellect, by an uncommon attachment to flowers [original note].

†*Julia to Anna Maria*: Judith Sargent Murray's daughter, Julia Maria Murray (1791–1822); Anna Maria (1790–94) was born to Judith's brother Fitz William (1768–1822), making the girl Judith's niece; *Salency*: a town in northern France famous for its spring festival in which a girl is named "queen of virtue" and crowned with a wreath made of roses.

———

THANKSGIVING.

AUTUMN receding throws aside,
    Her robe of many a varied dye;
And WINTER in majestic pride,
    Advances in the low'ring sky.
The lab'rer in his gran'ry stores
    The golden sheaves all safe from spoil;
While from her horn gay Plenty pours
    Her treasures to reward his toil.
To solemn temples let us now repair,
And bow in grateful adoration there;
Bid the full strain in hallelujahs rise;
To waft the sacred incense to the skies.

Now the hospitable board,
    Groans beneath the rich repast;
All that lux'ry can afford,
    Grateful to the eye or taste.
While the orchards sparkling juice,
    And the vintage join their powers;
All that nature can produce,
    Bounteous Heaven bids be ours.
Let us give thanks; yes, yes, be sure,
Send for the widow and the orphan poor;
Give them wherewith to purchase cloaths and food;
'Tis the best way to prove our gratitude.

On the hearth high flames the fire,
    Sparkling tapers lend their light,
Wit and genius now aspire
    On Fancy's gay and rapid flight;
Now the viols sprightly lay,
    As the moments light advance,
Bids us revel, sport and play,
    Raise the song or lead the dance.
Come sportive love and sacred friendship, come,
Help us to celebrate our harvest home;
In vain the year its annual tribute pours
Unless you grace the scene and lead the laughing hours.

SR [Susanna Rowson], *Boston Weekly Magazine*, November 27, 1802

————

THE HOPEFUL YOUTH.

A MAN who saw his son quite handy
Toss off a glass of strong French brandy;
Neddy, cried he, ah don't do so,
For liquor is our greatest foe.
But we are taught to love our foes,
Quoth Ned, so father—here it goes.

Anonymous, *Boston Weekly Magazine*, April 28, 1804

THE RETROSPECT;

or—ALL FOR THE BEST.

ONCE, ne'er was poor devil so maul'd by a wife,
 I'd a thousand times better been dead;
Ere sunrise, was wak'd by loud clamorous strife,
By mid-day she'd threaten to finish my life;
 And when twilight arriv'd—break my head!

Whilst a husband, good lack, how distressful my lot;
 I wish'd the cold grave was my bed—
I thought it were pleasing in quiet to rot,
To be nibbled by worms in mortality's pot,
 And no more fear the breaking my head!

Yet frankly I own, when my spouse was laid low;
 To be soberly stretch'd in my stead,
The blossoms of comfort, I thought still might blow,
I view'd the cold sod, quite content, that below
 Lay the bane of my peace—and my head!

    Anonymous, *The Fly; or, Juvenile Miscellany*, January 22, 1806

———

ELIZA . . . A *Poem*

In former times, when on Columbia's shore,
 Her sons had witness'd independence's birth,
When Massachusettes view'd the sterling ore,
 And with her patriot virtue stamp'd its worth,

There liv'd a soldier in true honour rear'd,
 One, whom proud Romans would be proud to own,
The majesty of arms in him appear'd,
 Mercy its crown, and Liberty its throne.

From his own breast each generous thought he drew,
 Its source untainted—the full stream was clear.
He sought not honour from exterior shew,
 But look'd *within*—and found the *soldier* there.

His sons in battle fought—in battle died,
    His country's freedom check'd each half shed tear,
One only daughter liv'd, his age's pride,
    Her form *enchanting*, and herself most dear.

The happy parents, fearing no disguise,
    Plac'd all their hopes on this their only child,
But fond affection often veils those eyes,
    Which reason opens to a mind beguil'd.

She lov'd—her parents—list this solemn theme,
    Hop'd in their bosoms was repos'd each thought,
Each tender sentiment, each passing dream,
    That could find welcome in a heart so taught.

Eliza lov'd—but love unfelt at first,
    Mantled her bosom—but with feeble rays,
Till on a sudden in full sway it burst,
    And dazzled reason with its flashing blaze.

Farewell to duty—farewell every thought
    That virtue sanction'd, confidence inspir'd;
Maternal fondness now no more was sought,
    Her father's virtues now no more inspir'd.

Her changing mind had warp'd her judgment too,
    Now, not her reason, but her fancy view'd;
She saw a soldier, and she *thought* him true,
    Because she *knew* her father to be good.

Stern virtue dwells not in external mien,
    'Tis but hypocrisy that's ever mask'd;
In low brow'd huts the native soul is seen,
    In loftier mansions is our judgment task'd.

No more each parent's anxious breast was nigh,
    The fond repos'tory of virtue's fear,
She shunn'd the car might startle at a sigh,
    She shunn'd the eye that might surprise a tear.

And proudly trusting to her strength of mind,
    She dar'd temptation, anxious to excel:
Without experience, to her weakness blind,
    Trusting she ne'er *could* fall—she trusting *fell*.

Anonymous, *Something*, April 28, 1810

———————

LORD DYRING . . . A BALLAD.

LORD DYRING about the land has strayed,
To seek for a fair lady bright;
And he has found him a winsome maid,
As ever blessed mortal sight.

Together for seven long years they lived,
Seven children their board surround;
Well they flourished, and well they thrived,
Till death made a dolesome wound.

This lady bright she is cold and dead,
And her husband did pine and plain,
But he sought another to fill her stead,
And he married a wife again.

He has married a maid, and brought her home,
But her heart was lordly and high;
As she entered the courts of the lofty dome,
The seven poor children stood by.

She took from the babies their ale and bread,
"Hunger and hate I'll give ye;"
She took from the babies their downy bed—
"The rough straw your bed shall be."

She took from the babies their bright wax light—
"Now in the dark turret go lay:"
The babies they wept the livelong night,
And they wept the livelong day.

Their mother, though pent in the darksome grave,
Heard their cries, from the lordly dome:
Leave of grim Death she has knelt to crave,
That to earth, that night, she may come.

So hard she begged, and she begged so strong,
That Death gave her leave to go;
"But I charge thee do not stay away long,
Come back ere the cock does crow."

The marble heaves, and the earth it opes,
And she comes to the upward air;
Her midnight path right on she gropes,
While her bones are stark and bare.

When near the castle she came, though 'twas dark,
And the mid of night had fell,
The dogs they raised a fearful bark,
They raised a mournful yell.

She entered so bold the castle hall,
Her eldest daughter stood there;
"Where are thy brothers and sisters so small,
Where are they, my daughter dear?"

"Indeed you're a woman both fine and fair,
But no mother, I pray, of mine;"
"How should I be fair, since the grave is my lair,
But I *am* a mother of thine."

"My mother was white, as the lily or rose,
Her lips, as the pink, were red";
"No white like the lily the dead e'er shows,
No bloom of the pink the dead."

She came to the tower where the babes did lie,
She kissed away every tear;
To the eldest daughter she says, "now hie,
And send the Lord Dyring here."

She dressed up *this* with a mother's care,
Another she brushed so clean,
Like a mother she combed the *third* one's hair,
And folded his ruffle so sheen.

When Dyring entered the chamber there,
She, in angry mood, to him said,
"I left ye plenty of food and fare—
My babies are crying for bread.

"I left behind down beds for the night—
My babies on straw they lay;
I left behind me the bright wax light—
Their room is not cheered by a ray.

"If I ever visit thee, Lord, again,
Woe, sorrow, and ill be thy share."
Then spake the new wife, "with might and main,
I'll watch for your babies' fare."

When the dogs bark, they still tremble for fear,
At the thought that the ghost is nigh;
When the little cur growls, they think she is near,
And shake till she passes by.

Anonymous, *Harvard Lyceum*, October 6, 1810

————

JEPHTHAH'S VOW.

The battle had ceas'd—and the victory was won;
    The wild cry of horrour was o'er.
Now arose in his glory the bright beaming sun,
And with him, the war chief his journey begun,
    With a soul breathing vengeance no more.

The foes of his country lay strew'd on the plain.
    A tear stole its course to his eye;
But the chieftain disdain'd every semblance of pain,
He thought of his child—of his country again,
    And suppress'd, while 'twas forming, a sigh.

"Oh Father of light," said the conquering chief,
        "The vow which I made I renew,
'Twas thy powerful arm gave the welcome relief,
When I call'd on thy name in the fullness of grief,
        And my hopes were but cheerless and few.

"An offering of love will I pay to thy name;
        An offering thou wilt not despise:
The first being I meet when I welcome again
The land of my fathers, I left not in vain,
        With the flames on thy altars shall rise."

Now hush'd were his words—through the far spreading bands
        Nought was heard but the foot fall around,
Till his lips in wild joy, press his own native lands,
And to Heaven are lifted his trembling hands,
        While the silence is still and profound.

Oh, listen! at distance what wild musick sounds,
        And at distance what maiden appears:
See! forward she comes with a light springing bound,
And casts her wild eyes in extacy round,
        For a parent is seen through her tears.

Her harp's wildest strain gave a thrill of delight;
        A moment she springs to his arms.
"My daughter! O God!" not the terrours of fight,
When legions on legions against him unite,
        Could bring to his soul such alarms.

In wild horrours he starts as a fiend had appear'd.
        His eyes in mute agony close—
His sword o'er his age frosted forehead is rear'd,
Which, with scars from his many fought battles is sear'd,
        Nor his country—nor daughter he knows.

But sudden conviction in quick flashes told,
        That daughter was destin'd to die.
Oh no longer could nature the wild struggle hold,
His grief issued forth, unconstrain'd, uncontroll'd,
        And the tears dimm'd his time wither'd eye.

His daughter was kneeling and clasping that form
 She ne'er touch'd but with transport before.
His daughter was watching the furious storm
That with quick-flashing lightning so madly deform'd
 A face beaming sunshine no more.

But how did that daughter so gentle and fair,
 Hear the sentence that doom'd her to die!
For a moment was heard the wild cry of despair;
For a moment her eye gave a heart-moving glare,
 For a moment her bosom heav'd high.

It was but a moment—the phrenzy was past:
 She smilingly rush'd to his arms,
And there as a flower when chill'd by the blast.
Reclines on an oak while its fury may last,
 On his bosom she hush'd her alarms.

Not an eye saw the scene but moistened in woe;
 Not a voice could a sentence command;
Down the soldier's rough cheeks, tears of agony flow,
While the sobs of the maidens heav'd mournful and slow,
 Sad pity wept over the band.

But fled was the hope in the fair maiden's breast;
 From her father's fond bosom she rose.
Mild virtue appear'd in her manner confess'd,
She look'd like a saint from the realms of the blest,
 Not a mortal, encircled with woes.

She turn'd from the group—and can I declare,
 The hope and the fortitude given,
As she sunk on her knee, with the soul breathing prayer
That her father might flourish, of virtue the care,
 Till with glory he blossom'd in heaven.

"O comfort him, Heaven, when low in the dust
 My limbs are inactively laid!
O comfort him, Heaven; and let him then trust,
That free and immortal the souls of the just
 Are in glory and beauty arrayed."

The maiden arose—O I cannot portray
   The devotion that glow'd in her eye.
Religion's sweet self in its light seem'd to stray,
With the mildness of night—with the glory of day,
   But 'twas pity that prompted her sigh.

"My Father"—the chief rais'd his agoniz'd head
   With a look of the deepest despair!
"My Father"—the words she would utter had fled,
But the sigh which she heav'd and the tears which she shed
   Told more than her words would declare.

The weakness was past—and the maiden could say
   "My Father, for thee I can die!"
The bands slowly moved on their sorrowful way,
But never again, from that heart-breaking day,
Was a smile known to force its enlivening ray,
   From the old chieftain's grief speaking eye.

Anonymous, Comet, Dec 7, 1811

———

THE CONSOLATION.

My goods are lost, my house is burnt,
   And yet upon my life,
No great misfortune have I met,
   For in't burnt my wife.

Anonymous, Boston Satirist, April 20, 1812

———

THE EFFECTS OF INTEMPERANCE.

BEHOLD the man! he once was famed,
For talents, learning, virtue, grace,
His wife, his children, and his friends
Were happy in his kind embrace.

But Oh! the change one vice has made!
Debased, despised, bewailed, undone,
His house no more the abode of peace,
His frightful race is almost run!

His wife with broken heart decays,
With grief his children hear his name,
His virtuous friends forsake his house,
And tiplers flock to drink and game.

The creditors begin to call
For debts contracted long ago;
Next comes the sheriff, seizes all,
And fills the family with woe.

To drown his cares, he drinks the more,
And hurries on with staggering pace;
He sinks in death, and leaves the world
O'erwhelmed in guilt, despair, disgrace!

Here let us pause, and warning take,
Draw back, and shun the enchanted ground,
Lest snares of vice enchain our minds,
Till no deliverance can be found.

A. K., Christian Disciple, March 2, 1814

―――――

TO THE AMERICAN GOLDFINCH.
Written by a late member of the Boston Theatre.

SWEET bird, how pleas'd I view thy endless care,
Thy mossy dwelling waving in the air!
How oft I mark throughout the livelong day
Thy course from bush to bush, from spray to spray!
O'er leafy trees, and wavy fields, thy flight,
To bring, before the dewy fall of night,
The sustenance thy unfledg'd offspring crave,
And only from thy ceaseless labors have.
On each return I hear thy constant mate
With twitt'ring wings, and melody elate,
Greet thy approach—and me thy golden breast
Finds, on the outward boughs a needful rest,
She from thy bill the welcome treasure takes,
And with her young a happy banquet makes.
Fond, happy bird, how envied is thy lot,

Thou from the youngster of the neighbouring cot
Art free, above his reach thy dwelling lies,
And safely screen'd e'en from his prying eyes,
Else might some murd'rous stone its firmness shake,
And quick distress and sure destruction make;
But thou art all secure—whilst I
Who gaze upon thee with a friendly eye,
And as I rest upon my labouring spade
Wishing kind heaven for me such home had made;
Know not what hour may tear me from the rest,
That could it last would make me ever blest.

Anonymous, Boston Weekly Magazine, June 14, 1817

————

THE ORPHAN.

Have you not seen the orphan child,
A helpless, friendless suff'rer cast,
Upon a rude unfeeling world,
Without a shelter from the blast?

Without a parent or a friend,
To wretchedness and mis'ry given,
To whom no kind protecting hand,
Points out the peaceful path to heaven?

Whose little breast can scarce contain
The swelling measure of his woe;
Yet smiles are mingled with his tears,
As oft instinctively they flow?

For yet, he knows not half the ills,
The sorrow, wretchedness and pain,
That lurk around his future path,
With their alluring deadly train.

With none to cherish, or to soothe,
Or sympathize in his distress,
And none of all the busy crowd,
If he were not, would smile the less?

Then what can life present to him,
But one unsocial dreary waste?
Vice spreads her toils—she lures—she soothes,
She flatters, and is then embrac'd.

And is there none to snatch, to save,
From this impending reckless fate?
And is there none, would nobly choose
To be *unfashionably great?*

Perhaps in nature's finest mould,
This orphan's infant mind was wrought,
Stamp'd with an energy of soul,
Form'd for the utmost stretch of thought.

His genius yet may force its way,
And stand unrivall'd and alone,
And nations tremble at *his* frown,
Whom *now*, the world scarce deigns to own.

For in that little breast, the seeds
Of immortality are sown;
A vast eternity's its claim
Though now neglected and unknown.

And there, perhaps, a dormant spark
Exists, which gently fann'd to flame,
Would throw a radiance o'er the world;
And spread the Saviour's glorious name.

And what can yield a purer joy,
A satisfaction more refin'd,
Than to protect the orphan child,
And cultivate his growing mind?

Anonymous, *Boston Recorder*, May 8, 1819

STANZAS

Addressed by a Lady in Vermont to her brother in the army.

Dear absent boy! though far away,
What anxious cares corrode my breast;
I bear thee on my heart by day,
By night thou art my constant guest,

I see thy young heart beating high,
In hope of glory, thirst of fame;
I hear the proud, ambitious sigh,
That flutters for the Hero's name.

I *feel* that patriotic zeal,
Which bears thee to the din of war,
And makes thee for thy country's weal,
Welcome the battle from afar.

But ah! the fatal hour is *here*!
I see thy keen eye pierce the foe!
As face to face, without a fear,
You aim the dreadful *deadly* blow.

Hark! Tis the awful cannons roar,
That makes the crazy myriads reel;
That bathes the earth in crimson gore,
And melts to wax the heart of steel.

E'en now in fancy's dreary way,
I roam among the mangled dead;
Where many an orphan's father lay,
Where many a breathless widow fled.

With tearful eye, and pallid cheek,
My lone step prints the crimson dew;
But ah! *that form*! I faint, I shriek,
O tis *a brothers' corse*[†] *I view*!!

Dread judge of heaven! in awful light,
Thou rid'st upon the raging storm,
Thy fearful judgements Lord are right,
And mercy shines in awful form.

Anonymous, Ladies' Port Folio, January 8, 1820

†*corse*: corpse.

———

A GRANDMOTHER,

TO HER INFANT GRANDCHILD.

O, go to sleep my baby dear,
And I will hold thee on my knee;
Thy mother's in her winding sheet,
And thou art all that's left to me.

My hairs are white, with grief and age,
I've borne the weight of every ill,
And I would lay me with my child,
But thou art left to love me still.

Could thy false father see thy face,
The tear would fill his cruel 'ee,
But he has scorn'd thy mother's woes,
And he shall never look on thee.

For I will rear thee up alone,
And with me thou shalt aye remain,
For thou wilt have thy mother's smile,
And I shall see my child again.

Anonymous, Ladies' Port Folio, April 1, 1820

———

A MOTHER'S LOVE.

A Mother's Love—how sweet the name!
    What is a Mother's Love?
A noble, pure, and tender flame,
    Enkindled from above;

To bless a heart of earthly mould;
The warmest love that *can* grow cold;
    This is a Mother's Love.

To bring a helpless babe to light,
    Then while it lies forlorn,
To gaze upon that dearest sight,
    And feel herself new born;
In its existence lose her own,
And live and breathe in it alone;
    This is a Mother's Love.

Its weakness in her arms to bear;
    To cherish on her breast,
Feed it from Love's own fountain there,
    And lull it there to rest;
Then while it slumbers watch its breath,
As if to guard from instant death;
    This is a Mother's Love.

To mark its growth from day to day,
    Its opening charms admire;
Catch from its eye the earliest ray
    Of intellectual fire;
To smile and listen when it talks,
And lend a finger when it walks;
    This is a Mother's love.

Anonymous, *Christian Watchman*, November 11, 1820

JOBS, SHOPS, AND THE PROFESSIONS

Early papermaking in New England
Courtesy of the Bostonian Society

In the "American Scholar Address," delivered at Harvard in 1837, Emerson urged students to move beyond books in their study of language:

If it were only for a vocabulary, the scholar would be covetous of action. Life is our dictionary. Years are well spent in country labors; in town,—in the insight into trades and manufactures . . . to the one end of mastering in all their facts a language by which to illustrate and embody our perceptions. . . . Colleges and books only copy the language which the field and the work-yard made.

Emerson's point gains support from the poems about work in this section, starting with the "MECHANICS SONG." Written by Benjamin Franklin (1706–90) for the July 4, 1788, celebration in Philadelphia of the ratification of the United States Constitution, the lyrics appeared, just after the visit to Boston of newly elected President George Washington, in the December 1789 issue of the *Gentlemen and Ladies' Town and Country Magazine*. In the process of extolling the labor of mechanics—that is, people who work with their hands often in specific trades—the poem provides examples of common jobs during the early national period. Far from exhaustive, it nonetheless includes tailors, masons, blacksmiths, shoemakers, cobblers, cabinetmakers, joiners, carpenters, hatters, coach makers, carders, spinners, weavers, coopers, ship makers, and sail riggers. Underscoring Emerson's point about language and work, it's worth noting that many of the terms in the "MECHANICS SONG" were connected to a number of other words, that "hatter," for example, was associated with such synonymous and subordinated terms as milliner, haberdasher, chapeler, beaver, felter, blocker, blockcutter, plaiter, and planker. Other poems included here focus on professionals and businessmen—lawyers, physicians, ministers, teachers, bankers, shopkeepers, and clerks—as well as people who engaged in miscellaneous or random occupations and pursuits, including actors, students, poets, hermits, booksellers, newspaper carriers, and street sweepers.

Although poverty would increase along with urbanization and industrialization in the early decades of the antebellum period, there is little sign of these trends in the earlier poems we found about work. Toward the end of our period, one starts to see more polemical approaches, as in "POVERTY" and "WEALTH," two poems that appear next to each other in the March 11, 1820, issue of the *Ladies' Port Folio*. The former bemoans the "chilling" effect of poverty on "Harmony and Love"; the latter sees the desire for riches as the fundamental moral problem of the age:

> For thee the merchant risks his all,
> While sorrows rend his breast—
> For thee, must empires rise and fall,
> And virtue be oppress'd.

The condemnation of avarice and materialism seen in these poems would advance both Christian and secular ideologies throughout the nineteenth century, but in the representative, earlier work collected here one finds a generally comic or light tone, at times satirical, at times celebratory.

As its title suggests, "MECHANICS SONG" jauntily embraces and advises workers who were busily constructing the new American republic. It begins,

> Ye merry mechanics come join in my song,
> And let the brisk chorus come bounding along,
> Tho' some may be poor, and some rich there may be
> Yet all are contented and happy and free—

and it goes on to assert the nobility of the trades mentioned by highlighting their ancient and biblical lineage. Thus, we're told that "the lord of the world was a Taylor by trade" and that Egyptian and Chinese masonry is still standing. The poem affirms both Franklinian industriousness for individual workers and the role of mechanics in forging the new nation:

> Ye Ship-builders! Riggers and Makers of sails,
> Already the new constitution prevails;
> . . .
> Each Tradesman turn out with his tool in his hand,
> To cherish the Arts and keep Peace through the land.

Considering the long tradition of lawyer-bashing (one thinks of Shakespeare's "first . . . let's kill all the lawyers"), it's not surprising to find conventional characterizations. In "On the multitude of LAWYERS," from the December 1789 issue of the *Massachusetts Magazine*, lawyers are said to breed like dogs, while several poems assail doctors and preachers. The familiar complaint about doctors (no doubt valid decades before the germ theory of disease was promulgated!) was that they were more likely to kill than cure. This is put succinctly in "EPIGRAM—TO A PHYSICIAN" from the February 18, 1804, issue of the *Boston Weekly Magazine:* "You say you doctored me when lately ill, / To prove you did not, I am *living still!*" A lament about how much doctors charge for their services appears in "LINES WRITTEN ON THE FRONT PAGE OF A DOCTOR'S ACCOUNT BOOK" from the July 7, 1804, issue of the same magazine.

Poems about ministers tend to highlight their didacticism, rigidity, or hypocrisy. In "ATIONS," which ran in the October 1796 issue of the *Massachusetts Magazine*, a sermon turns out to be not spiritual instruction but a political rant based on very recent news. In "EPIGRAM. WITH folded arms and uplift eyes" from the April 9, 1803, issue of the *Boston Weekly Magazine*, a minister who has just prayed for rain is caught, perhaps faithlessly, without rain gear when it starts to pour following the service. The poem that begins "In the fullness of blessing" is interesting both for the radical point it makes and its placement on the page of the August 1790 issue of the *Massachusetts Magazine*. Assailing organized religion as the worship of money (Mammon), it appears just above "On the CHOICE of a HUSBAND," a poem included in our section on men and women that rejects blasphemers along with drunkards and fops.

Poems about poetry as a vocation have a special resonance in an anthology of verse. In the background of these often-critical works stands the mixed legacy of Massachusetts-based, Puritan writers like Anne Bradstreet (1612–72), Michael Wigglesworth (1631–1705), Edward Taylor (1642–1729), and the ministers who created *The Bay Psalm Book* (1640). Although Bradsteeet stands as a foundational figure in the development of American woman's poetry, Taylor's rich and vivid verse was unknown until the twentieth century, and the didactic poetry of Wigglesworth and the psalm revisers has drawn little praise over the centuries. In fact, ridiculing the state of poetry in New England generally and Boston in particular became a familiar trope as early as Benjamin Franklin's seventh Silence Dogood essay, which appeared in the June 25, 1722, issue of the *New-England Courant.* Ironically promising to praise and encourage "poetic genius," Franklin famously applauded a particularly (un)worthy example:

> There has lately appear'd among us a most Excellent Piece of Poetry, entitled, *An Elegy upon the much Lamented Death of Mrs. Mehitebell Kitel, Wife of Mr. John Kitel of Salem, &c.* It may justly be said in its Praise, without Flattery to the Author, that it is the most *Extraordinary* Piece that ever was wrote in New-England. The Language is so soft

and Easy, the Expression so moving and pathetick, but above all, the Verse and Numbers so Charming and Natural, that it is almost beyond Comparison.

Franklin went on to insist that this elegy was incomparable and moving:

> I find no English Author, Ancient or Modern, whose Elegies may be compar'd with this, in respect to the Elegance of Stile, or Smoothness of Rhime; and for the affecting Part, I will leave your Readers to judge, if ever they read any Lines, that would sooner make them *draw their Breath* and Sigh, if not shed Tears, than these following.

And the lines he offers as evidence hilariously demonstrate that the poem is "extraordinarily" awful and likely to evoke tears of laughter:

> Come let us mourn, for we have lost a Wife, a Daughter, and a Sister,
> Who has lately taken Flight, and greatly we have mist her.

In an extended verse satire called "Boston—A Poem" (1803), Winthrop Sargent (1753–1820) offered the following overview of the kinds of poetry being published at the time:

> *Sonnets* and *riddles* celebrate the trees,
> And ballad-mongers charter every breeze.
> Long *odes* to monkies, *squirrel elegies*,
> *Lines* and *acrostics* on dead butterflies;
> Endless *effusions*, some with Greek bedight,
> And hymns harmonious, sweet, as infinite,
> So freely flow, that poesy ere long
> Must yield to numbers, and expire by song.
> *Elegiac lays* such taste and truth combine,
> The lap-dog lives and barks in every line;
> Each rebus-maker takes the poet's name,
> And every rhymer is the heir of fame.

These descriptions are both fair and misleading. Many poems by local writers included in Boston magazines were pretentiously highbrow and cloyingly conventional. But this collection demonstrates that some poems were strikingly modest and direct. In the few works in this section about poets, we encounter not "effusions" but sound advice and candid self-description. "THE POET" (from the *Ladies Afternoon Visitor*, January 10, 1807), for example, debunks the divine and, perhaps rising, Romantic view of inspiration by deflating ideas like these:

> That Poets blow dame Nature's flute;
> That on a cloud they sometimes ride,
> And go to **** without a guide;
> Live in castles made of air,
> And oft go snacks with Jupiter;
> That Philomel and they hold talk;
> That they with goblins often walk;
> That moon-beams are to them like fire,
> And they within them oft perspire.

Brought down to Earth here and in "*AN EPISTLE* TO THE EDITOR"—far from dining with Jupiter, chatting with Philomel, or walking with goblins —poets are seen as collecting their thoughts, "now and then, in leisure time" to share with interested readers. Similarly, the editor of *Something* reprinted John Maclaurin's poem "On Johnson's Dictionary" under a new name, "AUTHOR—ITY," from earlier publication in London because it assails what he must have seen as a still-current abuse of poetic license. Urging "young poets" to "take heed, / That Johnson you with caution read. / Always attentively distinguish / The Greek and Latin words from English," the poem offers a series of hyperbolic coinages as antidotes to what one probably shouldn't call Latinate pomposity.

Returning to the subject of trade and the experience of work, other poems in this section take us into shops by way of imagined conversations or verse advertisements. "Here comes Miss LIGHTHEAD," from the June 11, 1803, issue of the *Boston Weekly Magazine*, parodies shop talk when a customer questions the quality and cost of a fabric and a clerk insists that cheaper goods at another shop "will not answer." "ADVERTISEMENT" and "*ADVERTISEMENT* FOR ANYBODY THAT WANTS IT" provide inventories of merchandise at a fabric shop and a bookstore.

Two poems about education strike more serious notes. The author of "EXAMINATION," included in the *Harvard Lyceum* on September 8, 1810, effectively dramatizes the anxiety caused by taking a test and waiting for the results—a narrative undoubtedly based on his experiences as a student. And the author of "THE TRUANT," published in the November 16, 1816, issue of the *Boston Weekly Magazine*, laments the situation of teachers who are required, despite counter impulses, to inflict corporal punishment on disobedient students. The poem concludes with a useful and enduring point: that parents need to take responsibility for the moral education of their children, preparing them for school and supporting their teachers once they enroll: "Second his [teacher's] efforts . . . Nor spare their ear the true, unwelcome sound, / That misery from disobedience flows."

While no collection of work can fully represent life at this time, this section invites you to follow Bostonians into their workplaces, shops, churches, offices, schools, and manufacturing operations. Charles Sprague's "Good Folks, the Carrier! Fill'd with fear," published as a broadside by the *Evening Gazette* on January 1, 1816, is comprehensive enough to conclude this introduction. Charged with the task of writing a New Year's Day poem, the overworked speaker, a carrier, complies only after members of other professions he asks to do this refuse.

> I ask'd a *lawyer*—'he, indeed?
> 'He never scribbled but when fee'd';
> A learned *lady*—'she'd no time
> For ragged printers' boys to rhyme;'—
> To *Doctor Potion* next I went,
> And begged he'd give his muse a *vent*;
> But he, while out his lance he drew,
> Cried, 'dodge, you rogue, or I'll *vent* you'—

And so it goes until, driven by necessity, the speaker decides to write the poem himself:

> In such a plight, poor cast-off elf,
> I'd nought to do but—write myself!
> And though I feared my halting strains
> Would prove I had but scanty brains,
> Ev'n I, content my lines should show it,
> That though I ap'd, I was no poet,
> Mounted the nag, so oft by thousands jaded,
> And, pen in hand, lame doggerel's realm invaded.

While the halting rhythm that perfectly conveys the idea expressed in the last two lines suggests that Sprague was a better writer than he claims, the spirit of Boston's citizen poets—their inspirations for writing, the audience they addressed, and their sense of themselves as writers—is nowhere more clearly or charmingly captured than here.

MECHANICS SONG.

Ye merry mechanics come join in my song,
And let the brisk chorus come bounding along,
Tho' some may be poor, and some rich there may be
Yet all are contented and happy and free.
Happy and free, Happy and free,
Yet all are contented and happy and free.
Ye Taylors! of ancient and noble renown,
Who clothe all the people in country and town;
Remember that Adam your father and head,
Tho' the lord of the world, was a Taylor by trade.
Taylor by trade, Taylor by trade.
Tho' the lord of the world was a tailor by trade.
Ye Masons! who work in stone mortar and brick,
And lay the foundations, deep solid and thick;
Tho' hard be your labor, yet lasting your fame,
Both Egypt and China your wonders proclaim.
Ye Smiths! who forge tools for all trades here below,
You have nothing to fear, while you smite and you blow;
All things you may conquer, so happy your lot;
If you're careful to strike while the iron is hot.
Ye Shoe-Makers! nobly from ages long past,
Have defended your rights with your Awl to the Last;
And Cobblers all merry, not only stop holes,
But work night and day for the good of our Soals.†
Ye Cabinet-Makers! brave workers in wood,
As you work for the ladies, your work must be good;
And Joiners and Carpenters far off and near,
Stick close to your trades and you've nothing to fear.
Ye Hatters! who oft with hands not very fair,
Fix hats on a block, for a blockhead to wear;
Tho' charity covers a sin now and then,
You cover the heads and the sins of all men.
Ye Coach-Makers! must not by tax be controul'd,
But ship off your coaches and fetch us home gold;
The roll of your coach-made Copernicus reel,
And fancy the world to turn round like a wheel.
Ye Carders and Spinners and weavers attend,
And take the advice of poor Richard your friend;

Stick close to your looms to your wheels and your cards,
And you never need fear of the times being hard.
  Ye Printers! who give us our learning and news,
And impartially print for Turks, Christians, and Jews,
Let your favourite toast ever sound thro' the streets,
The freedom of press, and a volume in sheets.
  Ye Coopers! who rattle with driver and adz,
And lecture each day upon hoops and on heads;
The famous old ballad of love in a tub,
You may sing to the tune of your rub a dub dub,
  Ye Ship-builders! Riggers and Makers of sails,
Already the new constitution prevails;
And soon you shall see o'er the proud swelling tide,
The ships of Columbia triumphantly ride.
  Each tradesman turn out with his tool in his hand,
To cherish the Arts and keep Peace through the land;
Each 'Prentice and Journeyman join in my song,
And let the brisk Chorus come bounding along.

Benjamin Franklin, Gentlemen and Ladies' Town and Country Magazine, December 1789

†*Soals*: an alternative spelling for both soles and souls, hence a pun.

———

On the MULTITUDE of LAWYERS.

I WONDER William, Harry said,
From whom have all those Lawyers bread?
Quoth Will, I wonder at the same;
But Harry we are both to blame;
The more the Dogs the more the Game.

Anonymous, Massachusetts Magazine, December 1789.

———

EPIGRAM. [SINCE the *fulness* of *blessing* the *gospel* contains]
Upon reading (in the last Magazine) an Explanation of the following passage
— "The fulness of the blessings of the Gospel of Christ."

SINCE the *fulness* of *blessing* the *gospel* contains,
Is center'd in *money*, as witness'd by *Paul*;†

No wonder indeed then, that *Mammon* remains,
The *God of this world, priest, parish,* and *all.*

Anonymous, Massachusetts Magazine, August 1790

†*witness'd by Paul*: In the Jerusalem Campaign (Acts 11:29–30, Galatians 2:10, and Corinthians 1 and 2), Paul raises money for converted, impoverished Christians in Palestine.

———

THE *WHEN*, THE *WHY*, THE *WHERE*, THE *WHAT*, THE *HOW*.
EPITAPH
on an hermit

FOR years, upon a mountain's brow,
A Hermit liv'd the Lord knows how,
A rope and sackcloth did he wear,
He got his food the Lord knows where.
Hardships and pennance were his lot,
He often pray'd, the Lord knows what;
At length this holy man did die,
He left the world, the Lord knows why;
He's buried in this gloomy den,
And he shall rise, the Lord knows when.

Anonymous, Nightingale, July 12, 1796

———

ATIONS.
Not long since, as I was passing by a country church, where a large number
of people were assembled; curiosity led me to enter the house, where

I FOUND the congregation
In gaping expectation
Of the priest's declamation,
Whom they held in veneration—
He rose with moderation,
And, to my great consternation,
Instead of divine revelation,
He took the British Administration,
For the subject of conversation,
And said, the haughty nation

Deserv'd condemnation;
Who, without any provocation,
Had broken their obligation,
By the wicked depredation,
Made on our navigation,
Refusing to make reparation.
He then, with deliberation
Spoke of the Jacobin combination,
By whose instigation
That false representation
Was put in circulation;
Of the dangerous operation
Of the President's determination,
That there should be a ratification
Of Mr. Jay's preparation;
But to their mortification,
They met with a frustration,
Of which a full relation,
Would cause me close application,
And on a due consideration,
Make me mad with vexation;
Therefore 'tis my exhortation,
That they make proclamation
Of their humiliation,
For such a wicked inclination
To make an invasion
On the very foundation
Of the Federal Confederation;
And after an invitation
To the rising generation
To acquire a good education,
He made some deviation
From his former moderation,
And said he had expectation,
That these sons of abomination
By their national speculation
To obtain such a modification
Of Jay's negociation,
With the Senate's stipulation,
As they had in contemplation,

Would bring on ruination,
War, and devastation;
That in this state of probation
They should suffer starvation,
And their future destination
Be—Hell and damnation!!!

Anonymous, *Massachusetts Magazine*, October 1796

———

[Here comes Miss LIGHTHEAD and her tasty sister]

Messrs. GILBERT & DEAN

If you think the following, occasioned by reading the *Sapphics* in your
29th number, will answer for a Supplement, you perhaps will publish it,
when you have nothing better. If it be not so fortunate, as to "excite a
smile," it may shew some of your fair readers "their own image."

Here comes Miss LIGHTHEAD and her tasty sister;
Jack, off the counter, wait upon the ladies;
Show 'em what they call for, tell the price of each piece,
    Do your best to please 'em.

"Have you any cambrics, that are yard and half wide?
What's the price of that piece of tape-striped dimity?"
"Three and six-pence, madam"—"Let me see a better—
    Give me a pattern."

"Have you any stockings, very nice, with lac'd clocks?
What are these a pair, sir?"—"Madam, they're eight shillings"—
"I'm sure I saw much better, for only six, at FALE'S—
    They will not answer."

"I'll look, sir, at that lustring—is eight-and-six the lowest?
I'll give you seven shillings"—"That's less than what it cost, ma'am"—
"I'll give you seven-and-sixpence"—"Madam, you may take it."
    "I'll call again, sir."

May 28. CORNHILL

Anonymous, *Boston Weekly Magazine*, June 11, 1803

EPIGRAM. [THE young spendthrift *detests* the old covetous miser]

THE young spendthrift *detests* the old covetous miser,
Yet the miser's *well pleas'd* with the spendthrift: and why sir?
I'll tell you — the miser is very content
To *find gulls that will borrow* at twenty per cent.

Anonymous, Boston Weekly Magazine, October 15, 1803

————

EPIGRAM. [WITH folded arms and uplift eyes]

WITH folded arms and uplift eyes —
"Have mercy heaven" — the Parson cries,
"Upon our thirsty sun burnt Plains,
Thy blessings send in genial rains."
The sermon ended and the prayers,
Sir Cassoc for his home prepares;
When with his visage drest in smiles,
"It rains, thank heaven!" cries farmer Giles;
"Rains?" quoth the Parson, "sure you joke,
Rains? Heaven forbid — I have no cloak."

Anonymous, Boston Weekly Magazine, April 9, 1803

————

EPIGRAM — TO A PHYSICIAN.

YOU say you doctor'd, me when lately ill,
To prove you did not, I am *living still!*

H., Boston Weekly Magazine, February 18, 1804

————

LINES WRITTEN ON THE FRONT PAGE OF A DOCTOR'S ACCOUNT BOOK.

THE Doctor's fate is so severe,
He only *Duns* but once a year;
But when he asks the modest way,
The deuce, the devil and all to pay!

Anonymous, Boston Weekly Magazine, July 7, 1804.

THE MECHANICK PREFERRED.
An Epigram . . . Founded on a recent fact

One day lively Sue, at a female tea-drinking,
Says, Come tell me girls, for I have been thinking,
If we all had our choice to be married tomorrow,
What *business* in life our husbands should follow?
Why I'd have a Doctor, says Sally the witty;
And I'd have a lawyer, says Sophy the pretty;
Says Nancy the sober, from both these I pass on,
Give me, for my husband, the lovely young parson.
I am not so high-minded, says sly little Mary,
As to raise my ambition to men literary;
Those wise learned husbands to you I resign,
But give me, O give me, a COOPER for mine.

S., Polyanthos, April 1, 1806

————

THE POET

THE wise have long time held dispute;
That Poets blow dame Nature's flute;
That on a cloud they sometimes ride,
And go to **** without a guide;
Live in castles made of air,
And oft go snacks with Jupiter;
That Philomel and they hold talk;
That they with goblins often walk;
That moon-beams are to them like fire,
And they within them oft perspire;
And thousands still more strange than these,
But with them all we find they'll freeze.
Then now with patience let us seek,
And let us hunt with truth so meek,
Whether with fact these coincide,
And give due weight to either side.
First, let's begin then at the cradle,
Don't they suck pap then from a ladle?
Don't they crawl on hands and knees?
If well don't smile, if cold don't sneeze?

Their gums with teeth we rarely find,
No innate fancies in their mind;
In boy-hoods days and female hood,
(For oft the sex are poets good)
Won't they spit about and sputter?
And know what is and is'nt butter?
Crawl like snails to mistress scold,
And blush and mumble till they'r old
Enough to sing out *a b ab*,
And kick and storm like any mad?
Then send them off to any college,
Don't they grunt and grin for knowledge?
And do they love a lecture bell,
Or won't they scream out "are not well?"*
Next see them free from college rules,
An't they sometimes d****** fools?
I think I sometimes see them drink
And eat much oft'ner than they think;
And if to heav'n their souls take flight,
They leave their dust is dismal plight;
And though they live in air built houses,
Their bodies are the home of louses;
And thus like other men I shew it,
Is that denominated poet.

Zeuxis, Ladies Afternoon Visitor, January 10, 1807

*alluding to the excuse for indolence — viz. — "non-value" [original note].

EPIGRAM. [Boston stage]

'WHAT pity 'tis,' cries Crabtree in a rage,
'So much is squandered to support the stage!
To feed an idle, useless, worthless race,
Who else might aid the state, and not disgrace.'
'Nay,' Charles replies, 'no evils *we* create;
We choose the *refuse* only of the state;
Such as, from want of worth or want of wit,
For every *other* station are unfit;

'Tis such as these compose the *Boston corps,*[†]
Who must be FED, as 'players' or—'the poor.'"

Anonymous, *Polyanthos*, June 1, 1807

†*Boston corps*: actors at the Boston Theatre.

AUTHOR-ITY[†]

In love with a pedantic jargon,
Our poets now-a-days are far gone;
So that a man can't read their songs,
Unless he has the gift of tongues;
Or else, to make him understand,
Keeps Johnson's Lexicon at hand.
    Be warn'd, young poet, and take heed,
That Johnson you with caution read.
Always attentively distinguish
The Greek and Latin words from English:
And never use such, as 'tis wise
Not to attempt to nat'ralize.
Suffice the following specimen,
To make the admonition plain.
    Little of *anthropopathy* has he
Who in yon *fulged curricle* reclines
Alone; while I, *depauperated* bard!
The streets *pedestrious* scour. Why with bland voice
Bids he me not his *vectitation* share?
    Alas! He fears my *lacerated* coat,
And visage pale with *frigorific* want,
Would bring *dedecoration* on his chaise.
Me miserable! that th' Aonian hill
Is not *auriferous*, nor fit to bear
The *farinaceous* food, support of bards,
Carnivorous but seldom; yet the soil
Which Hippocrene *humectates*, nothing yields
But sterile laurels, and aquatics sour.
    To *dulcify* th' *absinthiated* cup
Of life, receiv'd from thy *novercal* hand,
Shall I have nothing, muse? To *lenify*,

The heart *indurate*, shall poetic woe,
And plaintive *ejulation*, nought avail?
    Riches *desiderate* I never did,
Ev'n when in mood most *optative*; a farm,
Small, but *aprique*, was all I ever wish'd.
I when a rustic, would my *blatant* calves
Well pleas'd *ablactate*, and delighted tend
My *gemiliparous* sheep; nor scorn to rear
The *superb* turkey and the *flippant* goose.
Then to *dendrology* my thoughts I'd turn,
A fav'rite care should *horticulture* be;
But most of all would *geoponics* please.
While *ambulation* thoughtless protract,
The tir'd sun *approprinquates* the sea.
And now my *arid* throat, and *latrant* guts,
Vociferate for supper; but what house
To get it in, gives *dubitation* sad.
Oh! for a *turged* bottle of strong beer
Mature for *imbibition!* and O! for
(Dear object of *biation*) mutton pies!

Anonymous, *Something*, February 10, 1810

†Reprinted from the May 1798 issue of the *Edinburgh Magazine*, where it was called "On Johnson's Dictionary" and copied from *The Works of the Late John Maclaurin, Esq. of Dreghorn* (Edinburgh, 1798).

EXAMINATION.

The authour of the ensuing effusion celebrates an event, and describes certain scenes, "quorum magna pars fuit."† As he is entirely unknown to us, we, as editors of the Lyceum, thank him for his communication, and fervently pray, that he is not one of the unhappy number whom he commiserates at the close of his poem. If we are not mistaken, he possesses a genius, which will not dishonour the poetick reputation of the college. He must indulge us in the liberties we have taken with his piece. We are prepared to defend the alterations and substitutions made in it by any mode of *private* communication or intercourse.

The morning sun on Harvard shone;
Loud sounds at six the clock's dull tone,

And many waiting younkers[†] own,
    Bosoms that throb most fearfully.

Now muster'd on the chapel stairs,
For the dread work each one prepares,
And face by far more woeful wears
    Than Quixote looking ruefully.

Called by divisions they obey,
And go, where leads the winding way,
A teacher, that looks stern as they
    Put on a face of agony.

Hard beat their hearts the livelong day;
They cannot banish fear away,
And faintly hope scarce darts a ray
    To dissipate their misery.

Haunted by day with fearful screw,[*†]
Th' approach of night rejoiced they view;
But evening hours no prospect shew
    Of end to their anxiety.

Next morning as the bell tolls eight,
Again on Harvard's steps they wait,
And while yet ignorant of their fate,
    The hours move on, how lazily.

But at the long-expected call,
With quick and anxious joy they all
Hie to the learned judges' hall,
    To hear th' awaited destiny.

Then quaking stand they all around;
Fix'd are their eyes upon the ground,
And (save the tutor's—hem!) no sound
    Disturbs the silent company.

How beats each burning bosom high,
As whispers *hope*, you're not turn'd by,

And how again it heaves a sigh,
    As *fear* but hints the contrary.

The answers given them, or make
Their throbbing hearts the fiercer ache,
Or thence the heavy burden take
    Which hung upon uncertainty.

Joy bursts from those, who not in vain
Have studied 'gainst this day of pain;
But others scarce their tears refrain,
    Who come prepared but carelessly.

Ah, hapless brothers, may success
A long vacation's study bless,
That you returning may possess
    A seat in th' university.

Anonymous, Harvard Lyceum, September 8, 1810

*We are sorry to find our young correspondent is so early initiated into the *technology* of college [original note].

    †*quorum magna pars fuit*: of which he played a major part (Latin); *younkers*: youngsters; *screw*: anxiety (?).

———

[Good folks, the Carrier — fill'd with fear]

Good folks, the Carrier — fill'd with fear.
In your dread presence I appear,
Grieving that I have sought in vain,
A *decent* 'New Year's wish' t'obtain.
But pray be kind — for through the town,
In spite of kick, rebuff and frown,
I've dogg'd the doughty rhyming band,
And bow'd and coax'd with hat in hand;
To old and young, female and male,
I've told my melancholy tale,
How all the live-long year throughout,
In head and cold I've jogg'd about,
And weekly trudg'd from door to door,

To give the fashions of the hour,
And bring the news as time roll'd on,
Of battles lost and kingdoms won —
But 'twas in vain — no soul would give me
A little doggerel† to relieve me.
I ask'd a *lawyer* — 'he, indeed?
'He never scribbled but when fee'd';
A learned *lady* — 'she'd no time
For ragged printers' boys to rhyme;' —
To *Doctor Potion* next I went,
And begged he'd give his muse a *vent*;
But he, while out his lance he drew,
Cried, 'dodge, you rogue, or I'll *vent* you:' —
A *merchant's* kindness then I courted,
Who with the muses sometimes sported,
But he, a crabbed, cross-grain'd d——l,
Beyond all others was uncivil,
And not content with stamp and frown,
With his large ledger knock'd me down.
In such a plight, poor cast-off elf,
I'd nought to do but — write myself!
And though I fear'd my halting strains
Would prove I had but scanty brains,
Ev'n I, content my lines should show it,
That though I ap'd, I was no poet,
Mounted the nag, so oft by thousands jaded,
And, pen in hand, lame doggerel's realm invaded.
My verse, you'll say, is wretched stuff
In truth, good folks, 'tis bad enough:
Much like the Carrier, very poor,
Just fit to hawk from door to door.
It comes for alms, and I would here
Have all in character appear.
And with the Carrier's bankrupt purse,
Match bankrupt wit, a greater curse.
So beggars, when they send a brat,
'Mongst feeling souls, for 'streaks of fat,'
Rig not on muslins, silks and laces,
But ragged coats with dirty faces.
'Twere well then, if my lines are dull,

Devoid of sense, of trifling full;
And, faith, they are most dull, 'tis true,
Witless and flat, tell nothing new,
Contain no slyly-slandering tale,
Nor ev'n at gadfly fashion rail;
They term no patriot party-slave,
Nor deck with stolen plumes the knave;
Nay more—they let religion rest,
Nor tell who's damn'd, nor who'll be blest—
'Twere well, perhaps, if wiser folks than I,
On this would pass their mill-stone visions by.
Now to its close my work advances,
And like the mongers of romances,
Who, when they're near their journey's end,
With wond'rous skill will comprehend,
In half-a-page or so, much more
Than volumes could produce before;
So I, who not at all have hasted,
But scores on scores of lines have wasted,
Had hit the mark, if I had chosen,
With ease in less than half-a-dozen.
As thus:

    Kind friends, the Carrier! pray befriend him,
And thankful from your thresholds send him:
We'll spend no words—for you and I know,
That all he comes for is the RHINO.[†]

Charles Sprague, Evening Gazette Broadside, January 1, 1816

[†]*doggerel*: bad or trivial verse; *RHINO*: slang term for money.

————

THE TRUANT.

As late I wand'red by the crowded school,
Where throng the num'rous sons of many a cit,
Till the press'd walls seem bursting from their bounds,
And the worn teacher's task, repeated oft,
And oft enlarg'd—beyond the labourer's toils,
Imprints the care-worn wrinkle on his brow:

The piercing cry of some poor hapless wight
Arrested by career. I linger'd by the door,
And heard the urchin, on the bended knee,
Cry loud for mercy—while the trickling tear
In briny streams, stray'd down and laved the feet
Of his offended master. Nor would he
Have sued in vain; but truant as he was,
Frequent the promises of reformation,
Had stay'd the hand of lenient justice.
And still should these prevail, for in the breast
Of him who executed his own sentence,
And reign'd the monarch of the buzzing crowd,
Humanity had fix'd her seraph throne;
Whence delighted she dispens'd her laws—
But precedent forbade; and the ferula
Suspended hung within the master's grasp,
Ready to fall in terrors on the wight.
And now awoke the painful struggle
In the good man's soul, between his duty
And sensibility's opposing power:
But justice must prevail, fulfilled must be
The law. The wise man's truth still held,
Nor would he *spoil* to *spare the child*.
It fell! But rather would th' inflicting hand
Endure the stroke, than give another pain.
But vain had been his counsel and advice;
Vain the warnings of his friendly tongue;
For nought were heeded all the threatenings
Of wholesome laws against such wand'rings made.
And thus holds out the law divine to man,
Terms charitable, friendly, just and kind,
Replete with goodness to a rebel race.
And man is urged t'accept the proffer'd good.
If, of the gracious invitation heedless,
He still persist in tracing mis'ry's path,
Then be the fault his own—On him alone
Will fall the dreadful curse, which nothing
Can avert.
    Think, parents, guardians, think! and ye who train
The youthful mind to virtue or to vice,

Consider well the tedious task of those
Who labour constant for your offspring's good—
And know, 'tis yours to render it pleasing
Or adverse: upon you it much depends
Whether the teacher lead with gentle hand,
Your children to the goal at which you aim,
Or by misrule at home, you give him cause
Of shame that he has yours beneath his care.
Second his efforts; let the precept flow
Frequent into your infants' tender minds,
Nor spare their ear the true, unwelcome sound,
That misery from disobedience flows.
Thus shall you plant the base so fair and strong,
The beauteous superstructure he will add,
Will catch th' admiring gaze of all around,
And make it a fit temple for that Pow'r
Who dwells on high amidst celestial stars.

Anonymous, Boston Weekly Magazine, November 16, 1816

Imitation of Martial.[†]

'Tis said, that great physician, Paul,
Who doctor'd and who murder'd all,
And so beat war and pestilence,
Has just become a priest—and hence,
Men in their graves by him are laid,
But still Paul hasn't chang'd his trade.

Anonymous, North American Review, March 1817

[†]*Martial*: Marcus Valerius Martialis (38–41 CE to 102 CE), Roman poet.

ADVERTISEMENT.

From auction just receiv'd, a heap
Of rarities, all wondrous cheap;
Of two cent Ribbons quite a freight,
Black, brown, red, olive, green and slate;

Long lawn for nine pence, which I'm bold
To say, is worth it five times told;
White cambricks extra fine and nice,
Too cheap alas, to name the price,
Broad cloths (importers sure are undone)
For less than sterling cost in London,
Hos'ry so cheap your time were lost in,
Cheap'ning any more in Boston;
Fine tapes (call soon or you will lose 'em,)
For only twenty cents a dozen,
Chintzes, of every price and kind,
From ninepence up to one and nine,
Seven pence for many a faded shawl,
And common gloves for—nothing at all.
For ninety dollars and no less,
One India cobweb muslin dress,
For beauty ne'er surpasse'd, howbe't,
The ladies will please call and see't
At No—, ———.
    N.B. Always on hand elastick garters,
Pins, needles, draws and other matters,
Too numerous for us to show forth,
So we must close with an &c.

Anonymous, Boston Weekly Magazine, January 10, 1818

———

ADVERTISEMENT.

FOR ANYBODY THAT WANTS IT

BOOKS, rare and cheap! and cheap and rare
    In State-street are for sale;
At half or double price, they are
    By packet, box or bale.

Bound and unbound, tied up or *loose*,
    (Licentious not is meant)
Here one can have his pick and choose
    At discount—no percent.

And here are *even* volumes *odd*,
    (Not strange or queer's intended,)
But such as never anybod-
    y, dead or living, mended.

Eternal, *ancient* works, which tend
    To guard us from all sinning—
Works which will never have an *end*,
    Which want, besides, *beginning*.

Here may the sage so studious pore
    On folios huge and many;
Some, with their covers gilded o'er,
    And some which have not any.

Observe the crowded shelves—and see
    The infinite variety,
One cannot help but suited be,
    (In physic, law, or piety.)

Call soon and buy—(wanted a Boy
    To read these books of knowledge;
Some clothes he'll have, and his employ
    Will fit the dog—for college.)

Part of a house to let—part cast
    For books, new, old, or strange:
And double the amount in trash,
    If taken in Exchange.

A catalogue made out—call soon
    No place so cheap in Boston:
Nor any where this side the moon,
    The wise no hint is lost on.

(Upstairs observe) also to sell,
    A Printer's apparatus,
Which, for a cent'ry has worn well—
    Pay—cabbage, or potatoes.

Guard 'gainst all bookstores else in town
    Whose cheats smell strong to heaven;
But well in memory write ye down
    The number 77.

Cape Cod Bard, *New-England Galaxy and Masonic Magazine*, April 23, 1819

————

AN EPISTLE

TO THE EDITOR.

Whether I shall be, or not,
A poet up to Walter Scott;
Or whether I've a right to hope
To write like Byron, Swift, or Pope;
Or ev'n in rhyming make a jingle,
Like the *starv'd* author of *Mc Fingal*;[†]
Or take a towering epick flight,
Like Homer, Virgil, Milton, Dwight;
Or o'er mount Pegasus so antick,
Like herds on either side th' Atlantick—
Admit no doubt—I'll tell you why;
Because, forsooth, I ne'er shall try.

But now and then, in leisure time,
For sport, I try my hand at rhyme,
And send on to your Ladies' Folio,
To eke out your poetic Olio.[†]

Some specimens I here enclose,
O'er which your patrons kind may doze,
Calmly, as though they were in prose.

Anonymous, *The Ladies' Port Folio*, April 22, 1820

[†]*McFingal*: mock-epic poem by John Trumbull (1756–1843); *Olio*: a collection of literary or artistic works.

PLEASURE AND THE GOOD LIFE

The Haymarket Theatre and Hatch's Tavern, 1798
Courtesy of Historic New England

At the start of the period covered in this anthology, Boston was rocked by disputes about the legalization of professional theater. Until the 1790s, a 1750 Massachusetts law banning the public performance of plays was enforced in the city except during the British occupation. As Heather S. Nathans explains in her study of early American theater, in part because theaters were associated with the British, in part because lingering Puritan and emerging Federalist suspicions raised anxiety about the impact of theaters on public morality, traditionalists like Samuel Adams (1722–1803) and John Hancock (1736–93) opposed the creation of playhouses. In August of 1792 members of the Tontine Association, an insurance and real estate development company, opened a five-hundred-seat theater in Board Alley. In a transparent effort to get around the ban, they named their theater the New Exhibition Hall but then proceeded to present plays, songs, and acrobatic acts. Outraged and determined to enforce the law, Hancock ordered Sheriff Jeremiah Allen (1750–1809) to close down the theater. It's no wonder that John Quincy Adams (1767–1848), at the time a young lawyer working in Boston, enthusiastically joined the pro-theater side. In 1792 he became an original stockholder in the Boston Theatre and published a series of letters in the *Columbian Centinel* making the case for its construction. Although the ban remained on the books until the early nineteenth century, Boston's first theater, a thousand-seat auditorium at the intersection of Federal and Franklin Streets, opened on February 4, 1794, and proceeded to present plays. Most of these were imported from England, but a few were written by Bostonians such as Judith Sargent Murray, Susanna Rowson, and William Charles White (1777–1818).

A similar, if less tumultuous, conflict smoldered around the publication of novels, another potential source of literary pleasure, in the 1790s. Widespread concern about their intoxicating and seductive power led novelists during the decade to insist that the stories they were telling were both based on true events and designed to bolster duty and conscience. Thomas Jefferson (1743–1826) caught both sides of the still-raging argument in his March 14, 1818, letter to Nathaniel Burwell (1750–1814):

A great obstacle to good education is the inordinate passion prevalent for novels, and the time lost in that reading which should be instructively employed. When this poison infects the mind, it destroys its tone and revolts it against wholesome reading. . . . This mass of trash, however, is not without some distinction; some few modelling their narratives, although fictitious, on the incidents of real life, have been able to make them interesting and useful vehicles of sound morality.

While poetry, as a venerable expression of high culture, did not meet the same resistance, the particular poems gathered in this section capture the anxiety about seeking pleasure for its own sake that underpinned quarrels about theatergoing and novel reading.

The Declaration of Independence asserted an inalienable right to the "pursuit of happiness," but whether this objective should be achieved through worldly pleasure or deferred gratification after death was a matter of concern. Because it celebrates the pleasure of quiet reading, it's appropriate that the first poem in this section is both called and addressed "To the Editor *of the* Town *and* Country Magazine." Secure and at peace with his books and magazines, the speaker offers this invidious comparison:

> Thus wrapt in my study, thus blest in myself,
> I never shall envy the miser his pelf:
> Let libertines revel, and monarch bear sway,
> I'm more easy, more safe, more happy than they.

A few poems here embrace the joys of love, some with cheeky wit, one with reverent appreciation. Examples of the comic approach include "EP-IGRAM. LAST THURSDAY, I MET WITH A SWEET SMILING SISTER," that ran in the December 31, 1803, issue of the *Boston Weekly Magazine*, "HEIGH-HO! BY A LADY," from the January 1, 1807, issue of the *Ladies Afternoon Visitor*, and "THE SINE QUA NON" from the February 9, 1811, issue of the *Cabinet*. The epigram kids around about the injunction to turn the other cheek; " HEIGH-HO" celebrates "the lass who fain would meet her swain / Nor let her parents know"; and "THE SINE QUA NON" jokes about (Cotton Mather, close your eyes!) Adam's fall:

> Oh! then laugh'd the landscape and garden around,
> And man blest with *beauty*, true happiness found;
> What our ancestor did all his children have done,
> And *woman* is still the sweet *sine qua non*.

A more earnest appreciation of marital bliss comes in "LIFE AND FRIENDSHIP" from the May 21, 1803, issue of the *Boston Weekly Magazine*, which begins,

LET Cynics and Snarlers continue to rail
At life, and pretend to despise every pleasure;
I know there are joys, whose source never can fail,
And life by enjoyment, alone will I measure.

Rejecting the view that "women are torments," the speaker insists that they have "charms, wit, talent, and beauty." All of these characterize especially the one he loves, Laura, who will, he's certain, be a treasure to the man she esteems.

Because "BACCHUS's SHRINE" (*Massachusetts Magazine*, January 1791) sees drinking as the ideal antidote for "mad despair," "gloomy care," "riot's voice," and "war's alarm," the range of human miseries it mentions casts a pall of desperate withdrawal over the promised relief:

While to my lips the glass I raise,
Hear my song of rapturous praise!
Thine is glorious fame for deeds
Worthy of immortal meeds.
Thou can'st conquer gloomy care,
Thou can'st conquer mad despair,
And the furies shun the shrine,
Where Bacchus revels blest with wine.

Other writers would clearly have looked askance at any celebration of alcohol. "PARODY," which appeared in the December 29, 1804, issue of the *Boston Weekly Magazine*, tells the story of a boy named Dick who drops out of school and into a life of drinking, swearing, impiety, and worse:

'Till seiz'd at last, for crimes to prison led,
Doom'd to saw stones, and live on mouldy bread;
Wear clanking chains, heave the repentant sigh,
Fearful of death, yet wishes oft to die.

A few allegorical poems take a broad, general, or extended view of the good life. "*PLEASURE*," which ran in *Ladies' Port Folio* on March 11, 1820, sees its eponymous figure as a "syren" whose "gay capricious power" holds sway in youth but changes over time as "glittering" delights give way to joy in the forgiveness of sin and hope for eternal life. In "*Time and Pleasure*" (*North American Review*, September 1817), "HOPE" (*Panoplist, and Missionary Herald*, July 1818), and "*TIME*" (*Christian Watchman*, October 2, 1819), beauty and joy contend with mortality and inexorably lose. "HOPE" features vivid images of this conflict:

> "I gazed—the lovely halo fled,
> And the blue flames that light the dead,
> Flash'd fiercely o'er a subtle cloud,
> No vision this—'twas Death's cold shroud.
> Thy charm is o'er—dissolv'd thy spell,
> To all thy fond deceits *farewell*!"

Though they may or may not represent the full range of ways pleasure and the good life were regarded in Boston during the early national period, this small group of poems suggests that 160 years after the Winthrop Fleet dropped off its passengers, having fun was still regarded with suspicion by many in Boston. This surely included the anonymous poet whose "HUMAN INCONSISTENCY, or, THE UNIVERSAL PORTRAIT" (*Boston Weekly Magazine*, December 10, 1803) sees the effort to have fun as part of a cycle that repeatedly leads to grief:

> Warm in the pursuit of pleasure,
> Deaf to warning and advice;
> Thoughtless, spends he all his treasure,
> Dup'd by every luring vice.
>
> From his dream of bliss awaking,
> Shame, perhaps, may sorrow force,
> Soon he virtue's paths forsaking,
> —Runs again his former course.

To the Editor of the Town and Country Magazine

WITH books on each hand, my fancy to please,
Secure from all strife, I sit at my ease;
'Tis here I in silence converse with the dead,
And wiser become as their precepts I read;
But when I would know what the world is about,
As who is took in, and who is turn'd out;
How love and intrigue, how fashion and mode
Among the *beau monde* are now understood;
I turn a quick hand to your Magazine,
And all in agreeable order is seen.
Thus wrapt in my study, thus blest in myself,
I never shall envy the miser his pelf:
Let libertines revel, and monarch bear sway,
I'm more easy, more safe, more happy than they.
My mind is at rest, I enjoy what I have,
No more of kind fortune I ever shall crave;
Would Heaven but grant me another request,
And make me completely contented and blest,
O! send me in some rural place a retreat,
In a box that's convenient, sweet, airy and neat.
Where I might indulge my humour, and spend
My moments in pleasure with books and a friend.

Anonymous, *Gentlemen and Ladies' Town and Country Magazine*, January 1790

————

BACCHUS's SHRINE

BACCHUS, merry God of fun,
Thy crown's a vine, thy throne's a tun;
Round thy fane the graces sport,
And the smiling loves resort;
Here they fly from ghastly care,
Here they fly from mad despair,
Safe they live so near thy shrine,
Protected by all conquering wine.

While to my lips the glass I raise,
Hear my song of rapturous praise!

Thine is glorious fame for deeds
Worthy of immortal meeds.
Thou can'st conquer gloomy care,
Thou can'st conquer mad despair,
And the furies shun the shrine,
Where Bacchus revels blest with wine.
Let the grave, the proud, the sour,
Dare profane thy pleasing power;

Let them sip from muddy rills,[†]
Drink that some cold cloud distills,
Theirs, be water, pride and care,
Theirs, is grief and mad despair.
Far from this delightful shrine;
Far from real joy and wine.

Let me ever here remain,
Midst the sprightly, jovial train;
Riot's voice is here unknown,
War's alarm, or misery's groan—
Here I bid adieu to Care,
To Envy pale, and mad Despair;
Ever near this blissful shrine—
Give me freedom, love and wine.

EUGENIO, *Massachusetts Magazine*, January 1791.

[†]*rill*: a small stream.

———

HUMAN INCONSISTENCY, or, THE UNIVERSAL PORTRAIT.

SURE of animals existent,
    Man affords the highest mirth;
Vain, capricious, inconsistent,
    To his burial, from his birth.

Bless'd, indeed, he is with reason,
    But by various passions tost;
So that oft 'tis, at a season
    When he needs fit guidance, lost.

Now by furious wishes hurry'd,
   Light he feels—he treads on air;
Now, by trifling crosses flurry'd,†
   Down he drops into despair.

Warm in the pursuit of pleasure,
   Deaf to warning and advice;
Thoughtless, spends he all his treasure,
   Dup'd by every luring vice.

From his dream of bliss awaking,
   Shame, perhaps, may sorrow force;
Soon he virtue's paths forsaking,
   Runs again his former course.

                           Anonymous, *Boston Weekly Magazine* December 10, 1803.

†*flurry'd*: confused.

———

EPIGRAM. [LAST THURSDAY, I MET WITH A SWEET SMILING SISTER]

LAST Thursday, I met with a sweet smiling sister,
I clasped her waist, and with rapture I kiss'd her;
The gospel, quoth she, I learn'd from my mother,
When *smote on one cheek*, I always *turn t'other*.

                        Anonymous, *Boston Weekly Magazine*, December 31, 1803.

———

THE GRUMBLER

COREUS unmarried, *grumbled* for a wife;
Married, he *grumbles* still, and lives in strife!
A child is wanted; Heaven the blessing sent;
Yet still he *grumbles*, still is discontent.
Why, what's the matter, Coreus? Worse and worse!
The seeming blessing's turn'd into a curse;
The nurse and midwife drain my pockets dry;
I've nought to keep the boy with by and by.
A purse he finds; yet now, as heretofore,

He *grumbles* on, "Had it been so much more,
I might have left off labour, liv'd in peace;
But so it happens, all my swans are geese."
He sickens; now he *grumbles* without doubt;
"When will my health return? my money's out."
Death came and struck him; at one fatal blow,
He sent him *grumbling* to the shades below.

Anonymous, Boston Weekly Magazine, May 14, 1803.

————

LIFE AND FRIENDSHIP.

LET Cynics and Snarlers continue to rail
At life, and pretend to despise every pleasure;
I know there are joys, whose source never can fail,
And life by enjoyment, alone will I measure.

The Stoic will tell you that pleasure and pain,
Alike should be scorned, nor disturb our repose;
I'd laugh at the latter the former to gain,
Though the thorn wound my hand, yet I'll snatch at the rose.

They warn us of falsehood, and folly, and pride,
And paint as chimera's both friendship and love:
Say few are the friends by adversity tried,
And affection but dwells in the nest of the dove.

That women are torments, the plague of man's life,
That wealth is the source of all mischief and evil,
That he must be wretched who once takes a wife,
And he who is wealthy must go to the devil.

But vain are their croakings, I never intend,
T'imbitter life's cup, tho' not filled to the brim;
The man who is honest I'll own for my friend,
And though scanty my portion divide it with him.

Then as to the women, why women have charms,
Wit, talents and beauty, at least there is one
Who tho' she must never be prest in these arms,
And though icy her heart, yet that woman alone,

Convinces me Stoics and Cynics mistaken,
Have snarled without reason, and railed to no end,
For the coldest would from his indiff'rence awaken,
Had he but a woman like her for a friend.

Heaven grant me of wealth such a competent measure,
That want may ne'er tempt, honour's paths to forsake;
And Laura's esteem, 'tis a blessing, a treasure,
Diogenes† 'self† might have wish'd to partake.

Assured of her worth, then to read chaste affection,
Express'd in each eloquent glance of her eyes;

He'd have banished at once ev'ry frigid reflection,
Own'd life had its pleasures, and friendship its joys.

CONRADE, Boston Weekly Magazine, May 21, 1803.

†Diogenes (412–323 BCE): Greek philosopher and cynic; 'self: himself.

———————

PARODY.

ONCE gay in youth, and free from anxious care,
DICK trudg'd to school, and heard the morning pray'r;
Each day mov'd on with health and pleasure crown'd,
And saw his playmates, joyous, smile around:
Till lur'd by pleasure, deaf to conscience call,
He left his school, his books, and gave up all;
Soon learn'd to drink, to lie, to swear and game,
And rose superior to the blush of shame—
Laugh'd loud at virtue as a common pest,
And made Religion mild, a standing jest;
Roar'd loud in taverns, bullied in the street,
And cast all law and order under feet—
'Till siez'd at last, for crimes to prison led,
Doom'd to saw stones, and live on mouldy bread;
Wear clanking chains, heave the repentant sigh,
Fearful of death, yet wishes oft to die:

Oft he laments the day he left the school,
To follow idle boys, and play the fool.

COLUMBIAN YOUTH! in downy pleasure bred,
Pamper'd by ease, by fav'ring fortune fed,
Attend to Virtue! All her ways are pure,
Sweet are her counsels, her rewards are sure;
From vice and folly early strive to fly,
And heave for poor repenting Dick a sigh.

Anonymous, Boston Weekly Magazine, December 29, 1804

———————

HEIGH-HO! BY A LADY

The ladies sigh, they know not why,
    'Tis not through pain or woe;
For whether glad or whether sad,
    They always cry *heigh-ho*!

The lass who fain would meet her swain
    Nor let her parents know;
Within his ear, that he might hear,
    Now whispers him *heigh-ho*!

Sometimes distress, as many guess,
    Occasion will bestow;
But yet the Miss in hours of bliss,
    Will utter an *heigh-ho*!

As joy o'er much, is often such,
    As makes our tears to flow,
So billet-deaux[†] with joyful news,
    Occasions an *heigh-ho*!

The married pair, devoid of care,
    While mutual transports glow,
With pleasure speak, for words are weak,
    By echoing *heigh-ho*!

Heigh-ho then means a word of pain,
    Or joys which overflow;
When lurking aught, the secret thought,
    Is hinted by *heigh-ho*!

Anonymous, Ladies Afternoon Visitor, January 3, 1807

†*billet-deaux*: love letter.

————

'THE SINE QUA NON'

WHEN Adam was stationed in Eden's fair bower,
The lord of the beast, of the bird and the flower,
He exclaim'd, tho' creation my sceptre may own;
To happiness still there's a *sine qua non*,†
    Sine qua non, sine qua non,
To happiness still there's a sine qua non.

Then Deity pitied the creature he made,
And sent in compassion a help-mate and aid;
From Adam while sleeping, he pluck'd out a bone,
And formed of the *rib* the sweet *sine qua non*,
    Sine qua non, &c.

Oh! then laugh'd the landscape and garden around,
And man blest with *beauty*, true happiness found;
What our ancestor did all his children have done,
And *woman* is still the sweet *sine qua non*,
    Sine qua non, &c.

The parson will hammer and stammer all day,
That life's joys are fleeting, and man is but clay,
Still, though not recorded in Mark, Luke, or John,
He *sticks to his text* of the *sine qua non*,
    Sine qua non, &c.

The lawyer, who labours and sweats in his cause,
And puzzles his brain in expounding the laws,
Quits the forum with joy, and, without *pro* or *con*,
Finds a *precedent pat* in the *sine qua non*,
    Sine qua non, &c.

Oh! tell us, ye heirs of Hippocrates' skill,
Ye men of the mortar, the pestle and pill,
What *drop* can encrimson the cheek pale and wan,
Like the *dew* from the lips of the *sine qua non?*
   Sine qua non, &c.

The poet may sing of the charms of the lyre,
Of Helicon's[†] fount and Promethean[†] fire,
Though his musick surpasses the Mantuan swan,[†]
Yet what is it all to the *sine qua non?*
   Sine qua non, &c.

Then fill up a bumper—let's drink to the smile,
That sorrow, misfortune, and care can beguile;
In life's chequer'd path may we gaily move on,
Ever cheer'd by the love of the *sine qua non,*
   Sine qua non, &c.

A Secretary of the Embassy, *North American Review*, September 1815.

[†]*sine qua non*: (Latin) something that is absolutely essential, needed; *Mantuan swan*:
the Roman poet Virgil, who was born near Mantua; *Helicon*: mountain in Greece, home of
the muses; *Promethean fire*: stolen from the gods and given to mankind by Prometheus,
who was severely punished by Zeus.

————

Time and Pleasure.

WHILE Time's vast car with furious force,
O'er Pleasure's fields its path pursued;
She tried each art to stop his course,
And thus rebuk'd, besought, and woo'd.

"How dar'st thou o'er my garden ride,
The haunt of beauty, youth, and love;
Thy iron wheels crush all its pride,
And fright the songsters from my grove.

"Look at the ruin thou hast made!
My Paradise is half defac'd;
Where thou hast pass'd 'tis all decay'd
All leafless, desolate, and waste.

"These brilliant flow'rs before thee view,
Whose odours all the air perfume;
For pity do not crush them too;
Spare me these few, for thee they bloom.

"Stay then awhile, and rest thee now,
Here in my bow'r thy dwelling keep;
I'll twine my roses round thy brow,
And lull thee in my lap to sleep.

"See Love and Beauty kneeling there,
To beg, entreat thee to remain.
Shall Beauty breathe a fruitless prayer,
And winning Love implore in vain?

"Why thus mispend thy precious hours;
What whim impels thy wayward mind
To fly from Pleasure's couch of flow'rs,
And linger when on thorns reclin'd?

"Why, why this hurry to be gone,
When all my bliss depends on thee?
Dear do not drive so madly on,
O stay one moment here with me.

"What, wilt thou go? — then I'll not stay,
Thy car shall be my blest abode;
I'll sing to cheer thy weary way,
And scatter flow'rs along the road."

Pleas'd with the sweetness of her song,
Time took the Syren for his bride;
But ere a year had roll'd along,
Disgust was born, and Pleasure died.

Anonymous, North American Review, September 1817

"GOD IS THERE."

The following sacred Melody was written by MRS. ROWSON *of Boston, and originally sung at the Oratorio performed by the Handel and Haydn Society.*

In life's gay spring enchanting hours!
When every path seems deck'd with flowers;
When folly in her giddy round,
Presents the cup with pleasure crowned;
When love, and joy, and young delight,
Give to the moments rapid flight;
Touch not the cup, avoid the snare—
Where'er thou art, think God is there!

When manhood treads with steps secure,
Then mad ambition throws her lure.
Behold! up glory's dangerous steep,
Where widows mourn and orphans weep;
And laurels on the hero's head,
Are stained with blood a crimson red;
Then, ere the battle's rage you dare,
Pause, and reflect that God is there!

When age, approaching, warps the heart,
And avarice plays its niggard part;
When self-love every passion stills,
And every finer impulse chills;
When to a suffering brother's cry
It shuts the heart, the ear, the eye,
Think, ere you leave him to despair,
God will avenge, for God is there.

And thou, who through life's thorny road,
Perplexed by care and sin, hast trod;
Whose heart has bled, whose eyes have wept,
On pleasure's couch while others slept;
Though now on life's remotest brink,
Poor, humble christian! do not shrink,
Though deep the flood, each doubt forbear,
Strong to support, thy God is there!

Susanna Rowson, *Christian Disciple*, October 6, 1818

HOPE.

I said to Hope — "illusive power,
Thy reign is past, *we meet no more!*
Thy voice is smooth — thy smiles are sweet,
Rich glories on thy temples meet;
Youth hangs bright roses on thy face,
Love weaves thy robe with magic grace;
But thou art vain — and false as vain —
The dazzling source of grief of pain!
My heart was sick — I sought for balm —
Gay bubbles danced upon thy palm,
I touch'd — the gilded vapors broke,
Light was the round, but deep the stroke!
May's blushing flowers wav'd on thy breast,
T'was there I lull'd my cares to rest;
But while I slept, a serpent train
Wound round my soul, and stung my brain.
Yet still I woo'ed the beam that throws
Such varied lustre on thy brows;
I gazed — the lovely halo fled,
And the blue flames that light the dead,
Flash'd fiercely o'er a subtle cloud,
No vision this — 'twas Death's cold shroud.
Thy charm is o'er — dissolv'd thy spell,
To all thy fond deceits *farewell!*"
I ceas'd — the tinsel cords that bound
Her airy form to Earth's dark round
Were burst in twain — she seemed to rise
On the light clouds that veil'd the skies,
In mild unwavering radiance drest,
Girt with a blood-besprinkled vest,
Borne on the cross — again she smil'd —
Again despair's wild wish beguiled;
Again I drink the rosy beam;
'Tis living light — 'tis Heaven's own gleam!
Again I press the purple flowers,
Rear'd in Gethsemane's dark bowers,
That flush the marble cheek of Death,
And fill the tomb with fragrant breath!

O! if cold sorrow clasp me round,
If clustered woes like grapes abound,
If the dark flood that Satan pours,
In circling horrors wildly roars,
And the bold shafts he dares to fling,
Tear from my heart each tender string,
Wedded by faith by love divine,
Hope precious *hope* shall still be mine!

Laurette, *Panoplist*, July 1818

———

TIME.

I saw him hasting on his way,
    And mark'd his lightning flight;
Where'er he mov'd, there stern decay
    Spread his destructive blight.
Rapid the gloomy phantom hied,
    Envelop'd in the storm—
His eye shone out in sullen pride,
    And fearful was his form.

I saw him grasp the Warrior's wreath
    Won in the gory fray—
The laurel withering sunk in death,
    Its beauty fled away:
That wreath was stain'd with bloody dew,
    Unhallowed was its bloom—
It met the phantom's chilling view,
    And bow'd beneath its gloom.

I saw him pass by Beauty's bower,
    And listen to her lay—
Around the spot was many a flower
    Blooming its summer day;
With icy heart the spectre came,
    Her lovely form compressed—
She met his lurid eye of flame—
    The tomb-stone tells the rest.

On Youth's warm brow his hand he press'd,
    'Twas cold as mould'ring clay—
He laid his arm on Manhood's breast,
    The life-pulse ceased to play.
His fell siroc* o'er NATURE pass'd,
    And low she droop'd her head—
Her blossoms wither'd in the blast,
    And all her verdure fled.

But hark! a mighty Angel's voice*
    Will publish Time's decease,
And Jesus raise the dust of saints,
    Which long had slept in peace!
Then, cruel Time, the friends of God,
    Rais'd high above thy power,
And sav'd by their Redeemer's blood,
    Shall live, to die no more.

Anonymous, Christian Watchman, October 2, 1819

*siroc: a desolating wind; Angel's voice: Rev. x. 5, 6 [original notes].

———————

PLEASURE.

MR. EDITOR, I discovered these lines, as I was journeying through the street, the other day, and as my eyesight is rather bad, I supposed that I had found something of great value. Judge then of my surprise, when I saw these verses. My first impulse was to throw them from me; but, on reading them, I discovered so much power of versification, that I send them to you. Charles Crabapple. Essex Street, Salem, March 3rd. 1820

When first fair pleasure smil'd on me,
And rais'd her syren melody,
Enchain'd I listen'd while she sung,
And on the dear delusion hung.
With rapture fill'd my youthful soul,
Made time's swift tide more swiftly roll,
'Till I should grasp the glittering prize,
She hung before my ardent eyes.
For still the gay capricious power
Referr'd me to some distant hour;

Call'd to her aid hope's practis'd cheat
To keep me kneeling at her feet.
I tusted to her promise light,
Unmindful of impending night;
But soon withdrawn her loving smile,
I mourn'd her deep ensnaring guile.
But why should I the tale unfold,
The tale of woe, so often told,
Of early hopes and blighted youth,
And treachery of fancied truth?
Though disappointment's frown severe
Shall bid my soul the future fear,
And weeping memory can but mourn,
The joys that never shall return.
Oh! yet thou loveliest child of Heaven,
Pleasure! in pledge of sins forgiven,
Bestow'd on erring mortals here
To teach them virtue to revere!
Oh, yet to thee my constant heart,
Shall turn, though pierc'd by sorrow's dart,
And when death ends each woe of mine,
Seek in the skies thy worshipp'd shrine.

Anonymous, *Ladies' Port Folio*, March 11, 1820

REBUSES, RIDDLES, ANAGRAMS, ACROSTICS, AND ENIGMAS

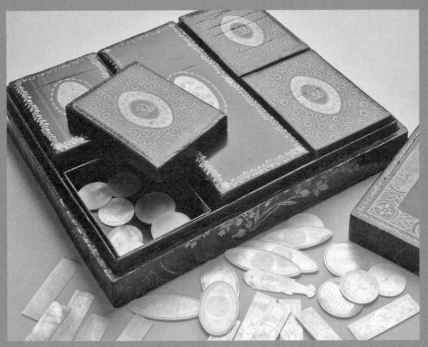

Game box with counters, 1790–1800
Courtesy of Historic New England

ach kind of verbal puzzle included in this section was imported into American periodicals from similar publications in England. Although the term *rebus* originally signified puzzles that use pictorial images to represent words or parts of words, the term evolved in eighteenth-century magazines to mean a poem that provided clues to letters or syllables that spell out words. As such, the rebus is a forerunner of the crossword puzzle invented in the late nineteenth century. A *riddle* generally asks a question that requires wit to answer and bases the solution not on an assemblage of individual letters but on an idea that makes sense of seeming nonsense. An *anagram* is a verbal puzzle in which the letters of a given word are rearranged to form a new word. An *acrostic* is a poem in which the first letters, syllables, or words spell out a word or series of words. As the Benedict Arnold and George Washington acrostics here suggest, acrostics in Boston magazines at this time generally employed the first letter of each line in their puzzle, with the rest of the lines adding themes and ideas. In the process of recognizing the poems' solutions, we learn that Arnold will live in infamy and broil in hell and that our first president is a luminous, historic bringer of peace and stability. Finally, an *enigma* is a general term for any kind of verbal puzzle. Less poetic than the other works in this volume, enigmas could describe any collection of objects, including the parts of a feast or a basket of flowers.

In a brief letter-essay called "On the Antiquity and Dignity of Riddles," addressed to the editors of the *Massachusetts Magazine* and included in their February 1789 (second) issue, one Q. S. defends "certain literary young ladies" whose "riddles and enigmatical questions" have been assailed by critics. These verbal puzzles, he insists, delight children and encourage their intellectual development. At a later age, he argues, college students should be taught the principles of logic by writing riddles themselves. The essay concludes with this flourish: "I would advise . . . beginners to adorn their productions with measure and rhime . . . [and] am happy to . . . advocate for an art that has frequently been held in the highest veneration by even Princes, Poets, Kings, Criticks, and Philosophers."

On the opposite side of the argument, in poems that criticized then-current magazine verse, it became conventional to rank rebus-writers among the worst offenders. In this way, the wag who scribed "Receipt to Make a Magazine" for the August 1796 issue of the *Massachusetts Magazine* included the following in his indictment:

A pointless epigram on censure,
An imitation of old Spencer,
A dull acrostic and a rebus,
A blustering monody to Phoebus.

If rebuses had been presented as candidates for literary immortality, complaints such as this would have been perfectly valid, since few, if any, are memorable as poems. But if they are seen as puzzles, games played by citizen poets and their fans who could become citizen poets themselves by submitting solutions, then these short verse exercises can be enjoyed as modest invitations to join an interactive, literary community.

In solutions that spelled out the full or last name of particular people, the rebus-maker could praise a hero, leader, author, or love interest. For instance, two of the most regular contributors to the version of the *Boston Weekly Magazine* that ran from 1802 to 1805—Judith Sargent Murray and Susanna Rowson—are praised in rebuses that appeared and were solved within five weeks of each other in 1803. Since both the rebuses and the solutions were published anonymously, we can only conjecture that these were expressions of mutual esteem written by each author about the other. More common are courtship poems, like "THAT part of the day when the sun brightest shines" inserted by Horath in the January 1, 1810, issue of the *Omnium Gatherum*. By working one's way through eleven clues on such topics as astronomy, mining, theology, history, geography, and zoology, the reader gathers letters that spell out NANCY CUTLER, and, as the solution concludes, "The initials of these put in order, disclose, / The name of a lady, more sweet than the rose." The rebus published by "B" in the March 1790 issue of the *Massachusetts Magazine* wraps its praise for the "worth . . . merit, [and] virtue" of one Betsy Cogswell in images of blooming flowers, verdant fields, and singing birds. Readers intrigued by these rebuses might enjoy following up on the names of the praised women by trying to learn more about Cutler and Cogswell—whether, say, they got married around the time the rebuses were published.

If a puzzle poem included here was solved in a subsequent issue of the same magazine, the solution also appears. Although poems that were solved can leave readers today wondering about how the solutions work, the unsolved or "orphan" rebuses we found are particularly fetching, tantalizing, even maddening! These poems may have been too hard to solve, or they may have appeared in the final issue of a magazine, denying potential solvers a forum for their responses. In either case, because they have lain dormant for more than two centuries, solving them would almost certainly require fascinating research into the history of American and Bostonian culture, broadly defined to include politics, history, philosophy, science, religion, the arts, social life, current events, and an expansive et cetera. And the process would definitely require resources like the *Oxford English Dictionary* and *Oxford Historical Thesaurus*.

The first respondents to these verbal puzzles may well have found them challenging, but at least they shared a general sense of the material world and cultural landscape on which the poems were based. For us, some two hundred years later, many things have changed. Clues that spell out specific words are often based on antiquated associations and images. For example, the acrostic solution to an enigma that ran in the February 27, 1819, issue of the *Boston Weekly Magazine* spells out the word "pen," but this solution makes sense only if we think of pens as feathers that are dipped in inkwells. The original solutions needed to mimic the poetic form of the rebus they solved, which means that just deducing the key letters now is not enough. Consider "An animal vain," an orphan rebus that appeared in the last issue (December 1796) of the *Massachusetts Magazine*. Even once we conclude that the town referred to in the final line is Boston, we may not be able to get all of the clues. While "baboon" is probably the animal in line one, and "Sabbath" the holiday "profan'd" by "moderns," guessing which exclamation beginning with an "o" (lines 2–3) and what "bard's estate" beginning with an "n" (line 7) is correct is more difficult. Twenty-first-century puzzle solvers, then, face a challenge the puzzle creators would never have imagined: we must read through long-dead eyes back to a time between the American and Industrial Revolutions. Delightfully, these poems add an element of playful problem-solving to encounters with Old Boston.

Perhaps because the *Gentlemen and Ladies' Town and Country Magazine*'s final issue appeared in January 1790, the issue that came out two months earlier in November 1789 contained two rebuses that were never solved in print as far as we can tell: "WHAT increases the sea" and "THE name of that earth." But first, to get you thinking about how to solve these puzzles, take a look at the "ENIGMATICAL BILL *of* FARE" and its solution. You can see that the solution is incomplete in that it provides answers to only twelve of the sixteen clues in the original enigma list. The clues are divided into four categories — meat, fish, vegetables, and drinks — but the solution omits the drinks, leaving them as orphans for you to adopt by figuring out what beverages available to Bostonians in 1803 could be described as follows:

13. A quibble, a numerical letter, and a consonant.
14. A Snare.
15. A young lad massacred.
16. One half of one of the four seasons, and a vowel.

To further whet your appetite for working on these puzzles, consider this short orphan rebus by one R. S. G. that appeared in the November 12, 1803, issue of the *Boston Weekly Magazine*:

> I AM both man and woman too,
> And go to school as good boys do.

Looks simple enough, but no solution ran in a subsequent issue. Each rebus implies the form of its own answer, and this one (by way of the "And" that starts line two) seems to call for a single word that has two meanings, that is, a word (or homonym) associated with both an androgynous, mixed, double-gendered, or gender-neutral person *and* the way good boys go to school. The second clue might be easier, since good boys, happy to go to school, might skip, smile, sing, or hum. Or they might do something specific to 1803 that children don't do now. Roll a hoop? Run backwards? Recite nursery rhymes or passages from the Bible? Practice declamation (arm gestures used in public speaking)? Hmmm. As for gender-mixed terms, these have changed dramatically since 1803 as more occupations have opened up for women. There are male and female doctors and lawyers now, but there weren't back then. When this rebus defied our efforts, we sent it to several people who regularly work on crossword puzzles. One of them, Paul Roberge of Exeter, New Hampshire, was stumped but suggested that if the word "good" in line two were "bad," the solution could be:

> Man or woman one may call a cousin
> And bad boys go to school a-cussin'.

And this led us to the following possible solution to the rebus as written:

> Each man and woman is surely a human,
> And good boys go to school a-hummin'.

Can we be certain that this was the intended answer? Definitely not! But you, dear reader, are invited to pick up where we are leaving off, not only with this intriguing, vexing orphan rebus but with the other unsolved puzzles in this section and in the magazines in which they originally appeared. And don't stop there. Solved puzzles also challenge us to understand how the answers made sense through imaginative reconstructions of life in Old Boston. By way of illustration, consider this clue and its solution from the rebus and solution that appeared in consecutive issues of the *Gentlemen and Ladies' Town and Country Magazine* in the summer of 1789:

One third of the instrument used of late
By LACO, to injure the head of state.

❖ ❖ ❖

A Pen is the "instrument used of late,
By Laco to injure the head of state."

A bit of research reveals that this "Laco" was Stephen Higginson (1743–1828), a Bostonian patriot, merchant, and Federalist who published a group of letters in 1789 assailing the then-governor ("head of state") of Massachusetts, John Hancock. Once you get to this Higginson, you could follow him to: the Continental Congress, which he attended as a delegate in 1783; Shays' Rebellion (1786–87), in which he played an active role; and then, perhaps, forward in time to his descendant, the estimable Thomas Wentworth Higginson (1823–1911)—minister, editor, abolitionist, Civil War officer, friend of Emily Dickinson and admirer of Poe—who in 1907 published the *Life and Times of Stephen Higginson*.

Read historically—with attention both to clues and solutions we understand and to ones we don't instantly comprehend—these verbal puzzles are doorways to knowledge about what Bostonians thought about everything from politics and current events to the food they ate and the people they loved. To encourage you to pass through these doorways by solving unsolved clues and understanding solutions on your own, no glosses are provided in this section. Getting past the confusion raised by these poems is, after all, the point!

A REBUS.

TAKE the sixth of a creature for mischief renown'd,
And a musical instrument join;
Then the name of a beautiful fair will be found,
Who the rest of her sex doth outshine.

R.G., *Gentlemen and Ladies' Town and Country Magazine*, April 1789

––––––––

Answer

A Monkey's the "creature for mischief renown'd,"
The musical Instrument's an *Organ*
And the name of a beautiful [fair] will be found,
In the amiable person of *MOR[GAN]*.

Hortensins, *Gentlemen and Ladies' Town and Country Magazine*, June 1789

––––––––

ANOTHER [Rebus]

Take three fourth of a creature which many admire,
That's often confin'd in a castle of wire.
Three fourth of a herb that the garden doth yield,
And a term us'd by husbandmen plowing the field
With that part of a swine that is now much in fashion,
And a town you'll discover in the *American* nation.

D., *Gentlemen and Ladies' Town and Country Magazine*, April 1789

––––––––

Answer

A *BIRD* is a "Creature which many admire,
That's often confin'd in a castle of wire"
Mint is "a herb the garden doth yield,"
And G's "used by Farmers when plowing the Field."
Ham is "part of a swine" at present "in fashion"
Thus *Birmingham's* your "Town in the American nation."

Hortentsins, *Gentlemen and Ladies' Town and Country Magazine*, June 1789

ACROSTICK

BORN FOR A CURSE to virtue and mankind,
Earths broadest realms can't shew so black a mind;
Night sable weal [veil?] your crimes can never hide,
Each are so great they glut the historic tide;
Defunct your memory shall ever live,
In all the glare that infamy can give
Curses of ages shall attend your name
Traitors alone shall glory in your shame;
Almighty vengance sternly waits to roll,
Rivers of sulfur on your treacherous soul;
Nature looks back with conscious ever sad,
On such a tarnish blot as she has made;
Lo! Hell receives you rivetted in chains,
Damn'd to the hottest focus of its flames.

Anonymous, *Gentlemen and Ladies' Town and Country Magazine*, June 1789

––––––––––

A REBUS.

TAKE two sevenths of the nymph of rivers and fountains,
One fifth of the season that darkens the mountains,
One third of a King turn'd into a swan,
Because he the death of a friend did bemoan.
Take also one third of the river most noted,
One half of a measure by Hebrews oft quoted,
One third of the instrument used of late
By LACO, to injure the head of the State
To which only add half the poem prepar'd,
To be sung at the Arches* the ladies had rear'd,
You will then have her name wrote before you complete,
In whose person the Graces have taken their seat.

I.G., *Gentlemen and Ladies' Town and Country Magazine*, July 1789

Arches: At Trenton-Bridge, in honor of the President of the United States [original note].

Solution

Mess'rs EDITORS,

I send you the following as a Solution of the Rebus in your last number

THE *Naiades* are "Nymphs of rivers and fountains,"
And *Night* is "the season that darkens the Mountains,"
Cyenus the "King, turned into a swan,
"Because he the death of a friend did bemoan."
Thames river, I take for "the river most noted";
An *Omer*'s the "measure by Hebrews oft quoted":
A *Pen* is "the instrument used of late,
By Laco, to injure the head of the state,"
And a *Sonata* the poem by some "prepar'd
To be sung at the Arches the Ladies had rear'd."
Nancy Thompson's the name then before you compleat,
"In whose person the graces have taken their seat."

Anonymous, *Gentlemen and Ladies' Town and Country Magazine*, August 1789

*Errata: in the second line of the Rebus, of which the above is a Solution; for one sixth, *read* one fifth [original note].

————

An ENIGMATICAL BILL *of* FARE.

MEAT.
1. Three fifths of a dwarf, roasted.
2. One of the northern constellations, broiled.
3. Israelitish food, in a pie.
4. Five ninths of a surgeon's instrument, roasted.

FISH.
5. The bottom of a Bay.
6. A Staff.
7. One of the five senses, changing the last letter.
8. Three fourths of a large house, a vowel, and three fourths of a mark to shoot at.

VEGETABLES.

9. Soot, and the offspring of a plant.
10. The nickname of a female, and three fourths of a woman of quality.
11. A Jewish measure, a consonant, and the duration of life.
12. A song of joy, changing the last letter

DRINK.

13. A quibble, a numerical letter, and a consonant.
14. A Snare.
15. A young lad massacred.
16. One half of one of the four seasons, and a vowel.

Anonymous, *Gentlemen and Ladies' Town & Country Magazine*, September 1789

Solution

Mr. Coverly,
I send you the following Solution to the Enigmatical Bill of Fare published in your eighth number page 436.

Meat.

1st A pig.
2d Bear steak, broiled.
3d Quail pie.
4th Goose roasted.

Fish.

5th Cod.
6th Pike.
7th Smelt.
8th Hallibut.

Vegetables.

9th Colly flowers.
10th Sallad.
11th Cabbage.
12th Carrot.

Anonymous, *Gentlemen and Ladies' Town & Country Magazine*, October 1789

ACROSTIC.

GREAT George's praise, each bard with rapture sings,
Emphatic great, compar'd to British Kings,
Our conquering Chief, who caus'd the war to cease,
Restorer of our Liberty, and Peace.
Guiding our councils with a careful hand,
Equal in Peace, or War to the command.
What firm foundation hath he laid for fame,
And time shall always waft along his name.
Scorning vain pomp, and mercenary pay,
He above monarch's, wing'd his glorious way.
In our west hemisphere hath rose a star,
Not Herschell's obscure spec, but brighter far,
Glowing with daz'ling light, the era's come
That does eclipse the heroes of old Rome.
On him we trust, whose virtue's his reward,
Nor doubt but he our sacred rights will guard.

Anonymous, Gentlemen and Ladies' Town and Country Magazine, November 1789

———

A REBUS.

WHAT increases the sea, and a part of a man,
Is the name of a place—which tell if you can.

Anonymous, Gentlemen and Ladies' Town and Country Magazine, November 1789

———

ANOTHER [Rebus]

THE name of that earth that's dug out of the ground,
And the place where in war-time a beacon is found.

Anonymous, Gentlemen and Ladies' Town and Country Magazine, November 1789

———

A REBUS.

THE crimson rose that blooms on Celia's face,
When modest virtue paints the lovely grace;
The fields where fancied Gods their bliss enjoy,

Whose fictious smiles gay fancy's tongue employ;
A flower bedeckt with beauteous hue,
Whose foliage fair distils ambrosial dew;
The sea born virgin of enchanting song,
Whose magick charms exceed the vernal morn;
A tint, that gilds the bosom of a mine;
The muse historick, fairest of the nine;
The tree, that breathes sweet fragrance in the grove;
Emblem of peace, of friendship, and of love;
The feathered songster of melodious lay,
Whose colour apes the blush of rising day;
That, which to nature gives her beauty round,
When Ceres smiles, in rich profusion crown'd;
A virtue, that adorns the female breast;
The fairest of the fair, by man carest;
The rose that decks the flow'rets of the lawn;
The messenger that hails the coming dawn.
The initials join'd, will *her* name disclose,
Whose mental charms excel the vernal rose;
Whose worth and merit, virtue doth approve,
To form a soul for friendship and for love.

Anonymous, *Massachusetts Magazine*, March 1790

———————

A SOLUTION *of the* REBUS *in the Magazine for March.*

BLUSH is the rose that blooms on Celia's face,
When modest virtue paints the lovely grace;
Gods in *Elysian fields* their bliss enjoy,
Whose fictious smile, gay fancy's tongue employ;
The *Tulip* grows with beauteous hue,
Its foliage fair distills ambrosial dew;
The *Syren* goddess sings th' enchanting song,
Her magick charms exceed the vernal morn;
Yellow's the tint that gilds the golden mine;
The muse is *Clio*, fairest of the nine;
The *Olive*, breathes sweet fragrance in the grove;
Emblem of peace, of friendship, and of love;
The *Goldfinch* tunes the sweet melodious lay,
Its colour apes the blush of rising day;

The *Sun* to nature gives her beauty round,
Where Ceres smiles in rich profusion crown'd;
Wisdom's a virtue in the female breast;
Eve's the fairest of the fair by man carest;
The *Lilly* decks the flow'rets of the lawn;
The messenger is *Light*, that hails the dawn;
The initials join'd will her name disclose,
Whose mental charms exceed the vernal rose;
Whose worth and merit, virtue doth approve,
To form a soul for *Friendship* and for *Love*.

Honorus, Massachusetts Magazine, May 1790

————

ACROSTICAL REBUS.

To the Editors *of the* Massachusetts Magazine.
Gentlemen,
*As the following Rebus has the necessary permit, you will
much oblige me by inserting it in your next Magazine.*

The bright inhabitants of realms above;
The name of goddesses of stream or grove;
A shining instrument each seamstress owns;
A blessing seldom found near royal thrones.
    Then take the justly celebrated name,
Of Ithaca's wife lord's illustrious dame;
The fields where pious souls in endless life,
Enjoy eternal pleasures free from strife;
The name of conduct generous and fair;
The splendid robes that kings and nobles wear;
The gentlest blessing mortals ever know,
Which dwells in scenes, remote from pageant show;
A country far renown'd for arts and arms,
Whose sons are blest with freedom's richest charms.
The initials join, and thus the name disclose,
Of her whose sweets excel the vernal rose,
Whose blooming countenance and graceful mein,
Whose soul refin'd, pure, virtuous and serene,
Demand the applause of all the virgin throng;
Whose merits are the theme of every shepherd's song.

Alonzo, Massachusetts Magazine, September 1791

SOLUTION to ALONZO's REBUS,
in the Magazine of September last
To the EDITORS *of the* MASSACHUSETTS MAGAZINE.
GENTLEMEN,
A few evenings since, two young ladies of this town, to amuse themselves made the Solutions *which accompany this. By their leave, I copied them, and request the favour of your publishing them in your next Magazine.*
I am, Gentlemen, *your humble servant.* A.B.

ALONZO! enamour'd of beauty and charms,
Which in bosoms divine raise tender alarms,
I pity thy fate if the maid prove unkind,
The maid for whom Doris and Damon have pin'd.
Tho' wrapt in a rebus with elegant art,
I soon found the name of the queen of thy heart.
Anna Pierce is the nymph whose good sense and merit,
Whose accomplishments, wit, and virtue and spirit,
Each shepherd admires and each fair one approves,
In whom are united the graces and loves.

ELLA, *Massachusetts Magazine,* January 1792

A REBUS.
MR. EDITOR,
By inserting the following Rebus in your entertaining miscellany and requesting a solution, you will probably gratify many of your readers, as well as oblige, your's, TIMOTHY TRIFLE.

An Animal vain, trifling and "spunky,"
Between the human race and Monkey;
A fashionable exclamation,
Of wondrous use in conversation;
A day our fathers highly priz'd,
Profan'd by moderns and despis'd;
A house at first that murders care,
Then leads to ruin and despair;
The first great law, by heaven made,
In our town meetings last obey'd;

Succeeded by a bard's estate,
A famous town will designate.

Timothy Trifle, Massachusetts Magazine, December 1796

———

A REBUS, *of which a Solution is requested.*

MESSERS EDITORS,

SEEING you have among your correspondents, some ingenius solvers of
Rebus's and Riddles; I send you the following.

Take one half of a crime for which millions have died,
With a portion of light for which thousands have sigh'd,
And you will find a *Boston* female's name,
Which ranks with *Rowe's* or *More's* in literary fame.

Anonymous, Boston Weekly Magazine, February 26, 1803

———

*[Out of the twelve Solutions to the Rebus in our last, we select the
following, as most poetical]*

In your Rebus, all readers recognize the merit,
In a lady whose talents and virtues inherit:
It is *Murder* the crime for which millions have died,
For one *Ray* of light many thousands have sigh'd.
MURRAY brightens our page with true classic lore,
And in justice, we rank her with *Rowe* and with *More*.

Anonymous, Boston Weekly Magazine, March 5, 1803

———

REBUS.

THE isle where Etna's flaming mountain stands,
The Grecian monarch who in foreign lands,
Roamed twice ten years: He who by hemlock died,
A statesman fair Columbia's boast and pride,
The youth who for his own fair shadow pin'd,
The stream whose real source none e'er could find,
Thetis's son whom nothing could subdue,
'Till at his heel the well aim'd jav'lin flew.

The founder of a great and mighty state,
The mount where fabled Gods held high debate,
What's more desirable than wealth and pow'r?
The flood which laves grim Pluto's dreary shore,
Heaven's first law by rolling world's obey'd;
He who the force of that great law display'd.

The initials combin'd,
And you'll presently find,
The name of a woman is shown;
By true genius inspir'd
By our sex lov'd—admir'd,
The honor and pride of her own.

Anonymous, Boston Weekly Magazine, April 2, 1803

————

ANSWER to *****'s REBUS in LAST SATURDAY'S MAGAZINE.

SICILY'S the isle where Etna's flaming mountain stands,
Ulysses the Grecian monarch who in foreign lands,
Roam'd twice ten years, *Socrates* by hemlock died
Adams, the stateman, fair Columbia's boast and pride;
Narcissus, the youth, who for his own fair shadow pin'd;
The *Nile*, the stream whose real source none e're could find;
Achilles, Thetis's son, whom nothing could subdue,
Till at his heels the well aim'd jav'lin flew.

Romulus, the founder of a great and mighty state;
Olympus, the mount where fabled Gods held high debate;
Wisdom, is more desirable than wealth or pow'r;
Styx, the flood which laves grim Pluto's dreary shore;
Order, heav'ns first law by rolling worlds obey'd;
Newton, the force of that great law display'd.
The initials combin'd,
And you'll presently find,
Susanna Rowson is shown;
By true genius inspir'd,
By our sex loved, admir'd,
The honor and pride of her own.

E., Boston Weekly Magazine, April 9, 1803

A REBUS.

I AM both man and woman too,
And go to school as good boys do.

R.S.G, Boston Weekly Magazine, November 12, 1803

————

THE RIDDLE—A NEW SONG.

I AM but a baby,
    I'm oftentimes told,
A sweet little bantling,
    Five thousand years old:
My nectar's a tear,
    My ambrosia's a sob;
I go with a frown,
    And I come with a throb.
My sweet little misses, pray don't you all know me?
I am sure, if you did, you would hasten unto me.

I speak with a smile,
    And I whisper a sigh,
I lodge in the heart,
    And I peer through the eye;
I dwell in a dimple,
    I play in the hair,
I rifle the bosom
    Whene'er I come there.
My sweet little misses, pray don't you now know me?
I am sure, if you did, you would hasten unto me.

I covet the dark,
    Like an owl or a bat;
I rove like a bee
    And I sting like a gnat;
I've wings like an eagle,
    And though I am blind,
I've a plaguy sharp eye
    To spy a girl's mind.
Then say, little misses, pray don't you now know me?
I am sure, if you did, you would hasten unto me.

Desire is my nurse,
    And Hope is my mother,
Occasion's my friend,
    And I don't want another.
I live at the sign
    Of the arrow and dove,
My nick-name is Friendship,
    My true name is Love.
Then now, pretty misses, since all of you know me,
Come make no more fuss, but hasten unto me.

COLLINA, Polyanthos, June 1, 1806

A REBUS.

THAT part of the day, when the sun brightest shines,
That part of the world, which is fam'd for its mines,
The author of mischief, who ne'er was found out,
The form of the belt, that girds Saturn about,
And that part of life best adapted for fight,
Will shew half the name I'm attempting to write.
Take the first christian emperour, sirnamed the great;
And the son of Laertes, that tossball of fate.
Take the name of a river, the pride of the Scots,
And the creature whose beauty consists in his spots;
Take the mimick, sent back to the horns by the hills,
And the fountain from whence flows perpetual ills;
The initials of these put in order, disclose,
The name of a lady, more sweet than the rose.

Horath, Omnium Gatherum, January 1, 1810

Answer to the REBUS, in our last number.

Noon's the time of day when the sun brightest shines;
The *American* world is most fam'd for its mines,
And for freedom far richer than mines that contain
The wealth of Peru, or the silver of Spain:
That author of mischief, the worst among foes
When mischief is done, 'tis *Nobody* knows.

A *Circle's* the form that girds Saturn around,
(May satan our foes in a circle confound!)
Youth's the part of man's life best suited to fight
In defense of our country, our freedom, and right.
Constantine the emperour was sirnamed the great;
Ulysses was reckon'd the toss-ball of fate;
Tweed's the name of a river, the pride of the Scots,
A *Leopard's* the beast of most beautiful spots;
An *Echo's* sent back to the horns by the hills,
And *Riches* are founts of perpetual ills.
The initials in order will truly discover
The name of a lady, so sweet to her lover.

Anonymous, Omnium Gatherum, February 1, 1810

———

ENIGMA.

Relentless foe of human bliss am I,*
At my blest lot lovers with envy sigh.
I feast on blood, and spurning all alarms
From those who seek my death, find life within their arms.

Anonymous, North American Review, March 1817.

Une puce (flea) [original note].

———

AN ACROSTIC.

Blessed news from every nation,
On thy bosom thou dost bear;
Sweetest tidings of salvation,
Through thy medium reach my ear.
O how charming the narration!
News of grace from far and near.

Regions, where the gospel never
Erst had spread Immanuel's fame,
Change their gods—embrace the Savior—
Overjoyed to hear his name.
Rising beam of gospel splendor,

Dawn afresh on *Christian* lands—
Every power shall soon surrender
Reins and scepter to his hands.

Orlando, *Boston Recorder*, June 16, 1818

———

*ENIGMA**

For knowledge I go, though nothing I know,
And by me is sent all the news of the day;
I taste now and then, after I have been,
Rubbing my nose every way.

*A solution is requested in our next [original note].

Anonymous, *Boston Weekly Magazine*, Februay 27, 1819

———

Acrostic—In Answer to the Enigma in our last.

Posses'd I am of worth, from the wing of Life I fell;
E'en in the richest Parlours I'm often found to dwell:
No one can be accomplish'd unless they use me well.

Anonymous, *Boston Weekly Magazine*, March 6, 1819

———

Origin of Life and Death.

	cur	fi	wr	d	dis		and p
A	sed	end	ought	eath	ease		ain.
	bles	fri	br	br	and		ag

Anonymous, *Christian Watchman*, June 19, 1819

———

ANECDOTE.

Old Harvard long hath stood—and in't
Once liv'd the famous tutor *Flint.*
On undergraduate catalogue,
Stood *Steel* and *Cotton*, *Trott* and *Fogg.*

It seems that, in those former days,
Some pupils follow'd crooked ways;
That is, would drink and make a noise,
Like some more modern college boys:
And, when they got "half o'er the bay,"
Would homeward take a zigzag way.

One night, *Steel, Cotton, Trott* and *Fogg*,
Attempted homeward thus to jog,
When they were met by father *Flint*,
Who gave *Steel* an ungentle hint,
That for this *row*, he did not like him,
But had a serious mind to strike him.

Steel cries, "hold, hold, if *flint* strikes *steel*,
Ignition *cotton* soon must feel;
And the whole four must quickly mog,
And *trot* away beneath a *fog*.

The tutor laughing at the pun,
Forgave them for their foolish fun,
And to their rooms unfin'd they run.

Anonymous, Ladies' Port Folio, February 12, 1820

DEATH

Landscape with tomb and urn, 1818–20
Courtesy of Historic New England

In this final section, a collection of poems that began with a young man's journey to the city concludes appropriately at the end of life itself—as it was imagined, pondered, feared, and embraced in poems published in Boston during the early national period. Like the cultural clusters represented in other sections, how death was understood was in flux during these decades. Archaeologists Edwin Dethlefson and James Deetz, who studied the evolution of gravestone decoration in and around Boston, found that the widespread use of death's heads lasted through the middle of the eighteenth century when they became less common than cherubs, which were, in turn, supplanted by the urn and willow motif that prevailed in New England during and long after the period covered in this book. While the adoption of the cherub suggests a more optimistic view of life after death, the urn and willow motif shifts the emphasis from the dead person's fate to a sentimental sense of loss. In *The Sacred Remains: American Attitudes Toward Death, 1799–1883*, Gary Lederman follows the shift away from the Calvinist "emphasis on human depravity that characterized the Puritan worldview [toward] a softer, sentimentalized imagination and religious sensibility [that] developed near the beginning of the nineteenth century."[1]

Although the poems we selected for this section can be read in the context of these large changes in religious ideology, each has its own voice and focus. A few works affirm the moderate, mercy-centered theology ascendant in Boston after the Revolution. Susanna Rowson's "HYMN FOR THE COMMENCEMENT OF THE YEAR," which ran in the January 2, 1814, issue of the *Christian Disciple*, celebrates "God's rich mercy." "THE RUINS OF AN OLD MANSION," from the July 17, 1819, issue of the *Boston Recorder*, moves from a detailed and deeply felt sense of nostalgia and loss brought on by revisiting a childhood home to the reassurance provided by the "lasting treasure" of eternal life: "From pain & woe, death soon shall grant release—/ An angel thou shalt sing to harps of gold." And two poems—"ON THE DEATH OF AN INFANT" (*Christian Watchman*, June 19, 1819) and "ON THE DEATH OF TWINS" (*Universalist Magazine*, November 11, 1820)—find solace in the concept of eternal life.

Two other poems—"*REFLECTIONS* IN A *BURYING-GROUND*" from the March 1796 issue of the *Massachusetts Magazine*, and the first version of William Cullen Bryant's "Thanatopsis" from the September 1817 issue of the *North American Review*—posit a world in which we cannot know much about existence after death. Both poets contemplate mortality. In "*REFLECTIONS*," death triumphs over "the embryo babe, the hoary sage, / And blooming manhood's intervening stage," while neither beauty nor genius can resist its power. Although the speaker alludes to the coming end of time and "unthought of" glory, this affirmation is toned down by the concession that in this world we see dimly, through an *"opaque medium* [that] veil[s] the skies."

The version of Bryant's "Thanatopsis" that is included here is far less upbeat and far gloomier than the later, better known text. In lines omitted in revision, Bryant criticizes poems that offer facile reassurance:

> In vain the flatt'ring verse may breathe,
> Of ease from pain, and rest from strife,
> There is a sacred dread of death
> Inwoven with the strings of life.

The closest Bryant gets to pious reflection in this first published version of his poem comes in the suggestion that the fear of death was inflicted on mankind at the fall: "And 'tis th' eternal doom of heaven / That man must view the grave with fear." The idea that dread is a part of God's plan and, therefore, sacred must in retrospect have seemed like cold comfort to Bryant, since the later version of "Thanatopsis" omits the reference to Eden lost and emphasizes the reassurance provided by nature. Similarly, in Moses Perkins's Romantic meditation "SOLITUDE," which appeared in the *Boston Recorder* on November 4, 1817, the speaker finds comfort in the tranquility of the landscape and in human virtue that helps him cope with "dust and the worm."

For comic effect or to express a quirky idea, several of the poems in this section avoid deep spiritual reflection. "ELEGY ON PERCEIVING A RENT IN MY OLD SHOE"—from the July 1, 1808, issue of the *Monthly Anthology, and Boston Review*—thus establishes a mock-heroic context for an extremely mundane event:

> Once was the time when tight and smart,
> My shoes defied the tempest's sway
> Till canker time, like Æneas' dart,
> Through two tough bull-hides forced its way.

Lingering over lost beauty and utility, the speaker grieves from top to bottom:

> Ill fated shoe, thy end draws near,
> With pain I view thy mangled form;

Sad is that heart, thou us'dst to cheer,
Cold are those *toes*, thou us'dst to warm.

A somewhat more serious line of satire runs through "THE OLD MAN AND DEATH"—from the April 7, 1810, issue of *Something*—which mocks people who, in the midst of suffering, "call on Death" but then cling to their lives. If Death appears,

They then no more pretend to sorrow,
But trembling, beg him call tomorrow;
Tomorrow comes, and Death appears,
Yet still they pray for future years.
Now future years have roll'd away,
Still, still, they sigh for one more day.

A more or less conscious adaptation of Jean de La Fontaine's (1621–85) poem "Death and the Woodman," which in turn was based on a fable by Aesop (c. 620–564 BCE), "THE OLD MAN AND DEATH" adds folksy humor and colloquial diction from its cheeky opening on:

'Tis strange to hear some people clack,
When hid behind their master's back;
But stranger still to hear some call
On death, that terror of us all!

Two poems express particularly unusual ideas. "*Written on the Author's* Natal Day," which appeared in the May 1796 issue of the *Massachusetts Magazine*, presents a speaker who dreads his birthdays because they remind him of his mother's death in childbirth and the general misery he has endured since. Impoverished and frustrated, coping with illness in his family, he contemplates his fate and cries out to God in prayer:

With more than usual haste this day is sped
With dangerous illness sisters are distrest;
The tears of anguish, and the throb of dread
Pain my swoln eyes, and rend my tortur'd breast.

God of my life! my darken'd soul illume,
Let me not murmur whate'er be thy will,
Help me o'ercome this unvailing gloom,
And under "chastening and rebuke be still."

As if students at some colleges should be treated by heaven with particular kindness, "To the Memory of William Henry Moulton"—from the September 3, 1815, issue of the *Harvard Lyceum*—bitterly offers this invidious comparison:

> SINCE death with ever jealous eye,
>   In youth's untimely hour,
> Has passed the vile and worthless by,
>   To pluck the fairest flower;

> Friendship may hang her mournful head
>   O'er a loved brother's bier;
> Nature may offer to the dead
>   The tribute of a tear.

If only to avoid ending on this sour note of unearned privilege, we'll turn to the more conventional treatment of death in *"Written in the Burial Ground, on Plymouth Heights, in Nov. 1818"* from the *Boston Recorder* of December 12, 1818. Like several of the works in this section, this poem draws on the English graveyard poets to make a point about New England. Standing on "consecrated ground," the speaker meditates in the dark, listens to the "murmurs" of the nearby ocean, and reflects on the revolutionary spirit of the Puritan "fathers . . . who burst the shackles of tyrannic sway." Along with bitter reflections on British intolerance and cruelty, this post-Revolutionary appreciation of antimonarchial resistance would become an enduring feature of how Bostonians and Americans at large came to remember the first Puritan settlers.

NOTE
1. Edwin Dethlefson and James Deetz, "Death's Heads, Cherubs, and Willow Trees: Experimental Archaeology in Colonial Cemeteries," *American Antiquity*, 1 April 1966: 502–10. Gary Laderman, *The Sacred Remains: American Attitudes Toward Death, 1799–1883* (New Haven, CT: Yale University Press, 1996), 53.

REFLECTIONS IN A BURYING-GROUND.

WITH reverential awe the turf I tread,
Where rest the "*sacred ashes*" of the dead.
Here lies sepultur'd many a charm unknown,
Whose germs were blasted, e'er the flowers were blown.
Here rest the embryo babe, the hoary sage,
And blooming manhood's intervening stage.
Here "*beauty's blush*" and *soul-electric* eye,
Whose smile was "fancy's heaven," inactive lie.
Here too its prostrate length must wisdom throw,
And where a *genius* blaz'd, a *thistle* grow.
Here shall they sleep, till bending time shall fall,
And in tremendous ruin bury all;
Chaos shall reign, creation's bounds shall shake,
And *time*, stern tyrant death thy scepter break.
Then shall the curtain of all nature rise,
Nor longer *opaque medium* veil the skies;
Th' Almighty FIAT burst the interring mound,
And *glories*, erst unthought of, beam around.

ESSEX, *Massachusetts Magazine*, March 1796

———————

Written on the Author's Natal Day.

EACH "birth-day" to devote to joy and mirth,
Is one of the first lessons infants learn;
I ne'er was taught it: mournful was my birth,
And mournful is its annual return.

Soon as the vital air this breast inhal'd
Misfortune seiz'd on my devoted frame;
Penury and woes have ever since assail'd,
And scarce has glimmer'd kind hope's feeb'lest flame.

SHE, whose dear relics sanctify the clod
To which affection frequent visits pays,
Was summon'd to adorn the courts of God,
Soon as her wretched son commenc'd his days.

With "sombre pencil," and with colors dark,
Fate has depicted each successive scene;
Tost on life's boisterous sea, the fragile bark
Seldom one twinkling star, ne'er a bright sun, hath seen.

By penury precluded from that height
To which ambitious Genius dar'd to soar,
Chill poverty prevents my eager flight,
And fancy dares indulge itself no more.

The future's *camera* discloses scenes
More dark, more gloomy than the past have been.
Save when *imagination* intervenes
And through the gloom AMANDA's form is seen.

At that lov'd name the *fancy* pleasure takes,
And smiles at views of happiness to come;
But soon, too soon, timidity awakes,
And nothing then is seen but *real* gloom.

With more than usual haste this day is sped
With dangerous illness sisters are distrest;
The tears of anguish, and the throb of dread
Pain my swoln eyes, and rend my tortur'd breast.

God of my life! My darken'd soul illume,
Let me not murmur whate'er be thy will,
Help me o'ercome this unvailing gloom,
And under "chastening and rebuke be still."

Thou canst remove the clouds which now impend,
And threaten to o'erwhelm my wearied mind,
But while I ask, my soul's best loves amend,
Cease then to murmur, heaven will yet be kind.

Perfect the goodness which thou hast begun,
And grant a gracious answer to this prayer,
With faith and hope, in thy beloved son,
Help me with fortitude *life's load to bear.*

Monimius, *Massachusetts Magazine*, May 1796

ON A CANARY BIRD,

Whose Mistress going from home for a few days was found dead in his cage the second morning after her departure.

HIS Mistress gone, poor little Bill—
    His wings in pensive sadness hung;
His soft melodious voice was still,
    Unless these mournful notes he sung.

"Ah Mistress mine, where art thou gone?
    Return! Return!" he plaintive cried;
Thus many an hour he made his moan,
    Till sick, of hope deferr'd; he died,

Poor bird, with thee I sympathize;
    Such pangs the feeling bosom proves,
That wrung with anguish hourly dies,
    When absent from the friend it loves.

Anonymous [Susanna Rowson?], *Boston Weekly Magazine*, November 13, 1802

———

ELEGY ON PERCEIVING A RENT IN MY OLD SHOE.

Invidious time, beneath thy power
    All nature hastes to swift decay,
From thee we wait th' ungrateful hour,
    That calls each fav'rite joy away.

Ev'n now, alas! I lose, forlorn,
    The lov'd companion of my way,
That oft my fainting steps hath borne,
    And watch'd my feet so prone to stray.

Ill fated shoe, thy end draws near,
    With pain I view thy mangled form;
Sad is that heart, thou us'dst to cheer,
    Cold are those *toes*, thou us'dst to warm.

Ill fated toes, when at your cost
    Through splashing gutters I must go,

I know not which bedews you most,
    Or tears above, or mud below.

Once was the time when tight and smart,
    My shoes defied the tempest's sway
Till canker time, like Æneas' dart[†]
    Through two tough bull-hides forced its way.

Now torn, defac'd, in woeful turn,
    No trace remains of beauty there,
Scarce shall the passing trav'ler learn,
    Their hue was black, their toes were square.

Sweet shoes, no more, in graceful sway,
    Shall waving silk your tops adorn,
No more the black-ball's dazzling ray
    Eclipse the pearls of dewy morn.

Nor ever more, in lively dance,
    Shall you admiring mouths distend;
No more on *right* and *left* to prance,
    One more cast off shall be your end.

Ye shoe nymphs, beat your leathern breasts,
    In handfuls rend your locks of thread,
Shed tears of wax from eyes opprest,
    And mourn your fav'rite offspring dead.

Anonymous, *Monthly Anthology, and Boston Review*, July 1, 1808

[†]*Æneas*: the hero of Virgil's *Aeneid*, who survives the Trojan War, travels to Italy, and founds the state that becomes Rome; *Æneas' dart*: In the *Aeneid*, darts are used as weapons that sometimes penetrate armor that can include layers of bull hide.

————

THE OLD MAN AND DEATH.

'Tis strange to hear some people clack,
When hid behind their master's back;
But stranger still to hear some call
On death, that terror of us all!

Yet should he kindly hear their grief,
And proffer them their wish'd relief,
They then no more pretend to sorrow,
But trembling, beg him call tomorrow;
Tomorrow comes, and Death appears,
Yet still they pray for future years.
Now future years have roll'd away,
Still, still, they sigh for one more day,
Till age resigns the very breath,
Which years before was ask'd of death!
Such ways remind me of a story,
Which I shall briefly lay before ye.
An Old Man once upon his back,
Sustain'd the burden of a sack,
Till growing weary of its weight,
He plac'd it by his neighbour's gate;
Then sighing gaz'd upon his load,
And then the long and tedious road
So choak'd with hills, and rocks, and thorns,
For fate had curst his toes with corns!
Then pond'ring o'er his wretched case,
The tears began to flow apace.
His troubled mind oppress'd with care,
At length, he droop'd in sad despair;
On Death he call'd to take his part,
And set at ease his breaking heart;
Now, quick as sight, grim Death appears,
And with these words salutes his ears:
"What dost thou want, old man, of me:
Dost wish, that I should set thee free?
Lo! here I stand, I heard thy calls,
Rest thou shalt find within my walls."
With trembling voice and wild surprize,
The old man thus to Death replies;
"'Tis true I call'd for thee Grim Death,
But not to take away my breath!
You see I have a heavy sack,
Pray lift it on my weary back!"

Touchstone, *Something*, April 7, 1810

HYMN FOR THE COMMENCEMENT OF THE YEAR.*

The opening year demands our praise,
To him whose power prolongs our days,
Unnumbered souls from life have fled;
Why are not *we* among the dead?

God's sovereign mercy kept our breath,
Or we had slept the sleep of death.
Shall we long-suffering love despise,
Or from ungrateful slumberings rise?

This year its millions will demand
To be entombed by sea and land;
Our turn *must* come—this year it *may*,
But who knows when?—perhaps today!

Are we prepared to meet the Lord?
Have we obeyed his heavenly word?
If not, to-day attend his call,
Give him our hearts, our time, our all.

For favors past, let thanks arise;
For sins, let tears bedew our eyes;
While God's rich mercy flows around
May ceaseless songs of praise abound.

Anonymous, Christian Disciple, January 2, 1814

*This letter has been admitted because the subject of it is of great practical importance. If the person, for whom it was particularly designed, or any other reader, shall be dissatisfied with the sentiments expressed, and will forward a well written and candid reply, he may expect that it will find a place in our columns. Ed. [original note].

———

To the memory of WILLIAM HENRY MOULTON, a member of the Senior Class of Harvard University, who died July 4, 1815.

SINCE death with ever jealous eye,
    In youth's untimely hour,
Has passed the vile and worthless by,
    To pluck the fairest flower;

Friendship may hang her mournful head
    O'er a loved brother's bier;
Nature may offer to the dead
    The tribute of a tear.

For, Memory, with busy art,
    Will o'er the heart strings play,
Wake tender strains, tho' full of smart;
    Nor let them die away.

Anticipation, with her train
    Of baseless hopes, will sigh,
To give her evidence again,
    That "all is vanity."

And fond Affection's tender care,
    Which watched the opening flower,
And shielded from the chilling air,
    Or covered from the shower,

Will mourn that it so quickly grew,
    Repaid her care so well,
Since as it prematurely blew,
    It prematurely fell.

Religion, Science, all will mourn
    To see so fair a form,
From every flattering prospect torn,
    And scatted to the storm.

Yet friendship may repress her sigh,
    For his aspiring mind
Has found a wider range on high,
    A prospect unconfined.

Death's wintry blast now sweeps the plain,
    His frosts now reign severe;
But spring will soon return again,
    And drooping nature cheer.

Peace, then, to Henry's precious dust,
    And oft as spring flowers bloom,
We'll weave a garland of the first,
    To deck his peaceful tomb.

Cambridge, July 25, 1815.

Anonymous, *Christian Disciple*, September 3, 1815

———

Thanatopsis.

NOT that from life, and all its woes
The hand of death shall set me free;
Not that this head, shall then repose
In the low vale most peacefully.

Ah, when I touch time's farthest brink,
A kinder solace must attend;
It chills my very soul to think
On that dread hour when life must end.

In vain the flatt'ring verse may breathe,
Of ease from pain, and rest from strife,
There is a sacred dread of death
Inwoven with the strings of life.

This bitter cup at first was given
When angry *justice* frown'd severe,
And 'tis th' eternal doom of heaven
That man must view the grave with fear.

    Yet a few days, and thee,
The all-beholding sun, shall see no more,
In all his course; nor yet in the cold ground,
Where thy pale form was laid, with many tears,
Nor in th' embrace of ocean shall exist
Thy image. Earth, that nourished thee, shall claim
Thy growth, to be resolv'd to earth again;
And, lost each human trace, surrend'ring up
Thine individual being, shalt thou go
To mix forever with the elements,

To be a brother to th' insensible rock
And to the sluggish clod, which the rude swain
Turns with his share, and treads upon. The oak
Shall send his roots abroad, and pierce thy mould.
Yet not to thy eternal resting place
Shalt thou retire alone—nor couldst thou wish
Couch more magnificent. Thou shalt lie down
With patriarchs of the infant world—with kings
The powerful of the earth—the wise, the good,
Fair forms, and hoary seers of ages past,
All in one mighty sepulchre. The hills,
Rock-ribb'd and ancient as the sun, the vales
Stretching in pensive quietness between;
The venerable woods—the floods that move
In majesty, and the complaining brooks,
That wind among the meads, and make them green,
Are but the solemn decorations all,
Of the great tomb of man. The golden sun,
The planets, all the infinite host of heaven
Are glowing on the sad abodes of death,
Through the still lapse of ages. All that tread
The globe are but a handful to the tribes
That slumber in its bosom. Take the wings
Of morning—and the Borean desert pierce—
Or lose thyself in the continuous woods
That veil Oregan, where he hears no sound
Save his own dashings—yet—the dead are there,
And millions in those solitudes, since first
The flight of years began, have laid them down
In their last sleep—the dead reign there alone.
So shalt thou rest—and what if thou shalt fall
Unnoticed by the living—and no friend
Take note of thy departure? Thousands more
Will share thy destiny. The tittering world
Dance to the grave. The busy brood of care
Plod on, and each one chases as before
His favourite phantom. Yet all these shall leave
Their mirth and their employments, and shall come
And make their bed with thee!

Anonymous [William Cullen Bryant], *North American Review*, September 1817

SOLITUDE

The moon was retiring in clouds of the west,
And her beautiful lustre was fading away.
The foliage was ripe with a silvery crest,
Which deepen'd the shades, in which nature was drest,
As if mourning the absence of day.

I was charm'd with the landscape, which varied its hue,
As the glimmering light palely shone o'er the lea.
The shadowy clouds which skirted the blue,
Had sprinkled the verdure, with freshening dew,
And sunk to their rest on the sea.

Not a breath, with the sigh of the captive to soar,
Or a zephyr to dimple the face of the stream.
Save the far distant cataract's tremulous roar,
Or the echo of waves as they break on the shore.
It was silent and calmly serene.

And long, I exclaimed, may this solitude reign,
And the clamors of power and rivalry cease;
May the clank of captivity's wearisome chain,
And the battle's rude din, on the gore mantled plain,
Be hush'd in the slumbers of peace.

Then I mus'd on the years which long have roll'd by,
And the schemes which ambition and vanity form,
While the fate of true genius excited a sigh,
Left to flourish unseen, in obscurity die,
And mingle with dust and the worm.

But I felt that whatever stern fate should decree,
Still *Virtue* triumphant must flourish and thrive,
Though empires should totter and nations should bleed,
And whirlwinds destruction swift onwards should lead,
This—the wreck of the world should survive.

Moses Perkins, *Boston Recorder*, November 4, 1817

Written in the Burial Ground, on Plymouth Heights, in Nov. 1818.

I stood upon that consecrated ground,
Where in sepulchral state our fathers lie,
Night threw her sable drapery around,
And twilight trembled in the western sky.

Hill, dale, and ocean, faded from the view,
Blending their features in unvarying shade,
Nor seem'd less lovely in this dusky hue,
Than in the sun-beams glowing tints array'd.

The distant murmurs of the swelling deep,
Were feeble echos of its surging roar,
Which seem'd to lull its weary waves to sleep,
Upon the pillow of the spreading shore.

By some attraction to the spot confin'd,
I felt sensations quite unknown before,
Which imaged on the mirror of the mind,
The sacred forms, which peopled once this shore.

Two hundred years, their "cloudy wings expand,"
On that suspicious and eventful day,
When first our fathers landed on this strand,
And burst the shackles of tyrannic sway.

This fond remembrance flash'd upon my mind,
And like enchantment, held me to the spot,
Where mem'ry loves to linger far behind,
On names illustrious, now perhaps forgot.

It is a pleasure, mingled with regret,
To pierce the gloom of ages far behind,
Although the splendor of their orbs has set,
Yet still its twilight rests upon the mind.

These monuments, to future times shall tell
The bold achievements of our sainted sires,
And grateful thousands shall their requiem swell,
Till life, till liberty itself expires.

New-England's Parent guards their sacred dust,
And cherishes the emulative flame,
Which kindled in those patriot bosoms first,
Whose deeds are stampt with an immortal fame.

P., Boston Recorder, December 12, 1818

———

Epitaph on a tomb stone in a church yard near Boston.

As I was bid to drive the Horse,
Not thinking death nor danger near,
Until the Horse let drive his foot,
Which broke my Scull without his fear.

Anonymous, Boston Weekly Magazine, March 13, 1819

———

ON THE DEATH OF AN INFANT.

When the Archangel's trump shall blow,
And souls to bodies join,
Millions shall wish their lives below
Had been as short as thine.

Anonymous, Christian Watchman, June 19, 1819

———

THE RUINS OF AN OLD MANSION.

All wasting time! how has thy ruthless hand,
Swept roughly o'er the spot I once lov'd dear!
Where now the peaceful mansion that did stand—
Ah! what a mournful pile of ruins there!
No smoke above the trees winds gracefully;
Cold is the hearth where blaz'd the cheerful fire;
A lonely chimney meets the distant eye,
The wintry winds sad-murmur and retire.

No jealous dog announces my approach,
No inmate flies to greet me welcome in—
A solemn stillness reigns! Death's icy touch
Hath froze the tide that flow'd in ev'ry vein.
Ye woodbines where are ye? ye roses where?
That grac'd the walls fantastically wild;
That breath'd sweet fragrance on the healthful air,
And with your beauties sooth'd the restless child.
Say did ye wither mid the gloomy waste,
Forgotten by the hand that plac'd ye there?
Or did some careless hind, with cruel haste
O'erwhelm ye deep beneath the ruins drear?
Where is the ancient oak, whose branching arms
The red-breast sought to build her airy nest?
Secure from fear but truant boys' alarms,
And I did climb to break her peaceful rest.
All gone! ah me! what sadness fills the mind,
While pausing on the scenes of happier days;
The golden hours fly swifter than the wind,
And leave a cup of woes no joy allays!
Here did the matron spread the welcome board
Well pleas'd with friends her best repast to share.
Her smiles were joy, peace flow'd from ev'ry word,
Time stole away without one cankering care.
There by that *broken hearth* I us'd to hear,
With wondering eyes, the war-worn soldier tell
On winter's eve the enchanting tales of war;
How *here* the freeman triumph'd—*there* he fell!
The warriors fallen in the war of death,
To dust is turn'd the tongue that spake of wars—
What changes wait on every instant breath!
O earth! what giv'st thou but false hopes & tears!
Then, O my soul, look not for bliss on earth;
Earth will deceive thy hopes—entomb thy joys.
There's nothing here that suits thy heav'nly birth,
Why should a mind immortal sport with toys?
Ungrasp thy hold on sublunary things,
And seek a lasting treasure in the skies.
Who there arrives no more of sorrow sings,
But drinks unmingled joy that never dies!

So may'st thou smile at woe—with inward peace
Look out upon the storms that rock the world!
From pain and woe, death soon shall grant release—
An *angel** thou shalt sing to harps of gold!

Y.C., *Boston Recorder*, July 17, 1819

*Luke xx. 36 [original note].

———

The Maniac's last ray of reason.

O! Christ the fearful dream is past,
And "reason's ray" has dawned at last;
When shall my anguish'd spirit soar
To scenes of bliss on Eden's shore?
Angel of mercy hear my prayer,
Be thou the wretched Maniac's care.

Nights of horror and days of woe,
Embitter every hour below,
Whilst grief and agony combin'd,
Distract my anxious, phrenzied mind.
The wreck of reason now appears,
Triumphant o'er the wreck of years.

The storm is stayed the calm is come,
Welcome Elysium's joy and home.
Bound, parting spirit, through thy clay,
From night of gloom to endless day.
A gleam of glory round him shone,
And soul and sorrows both were gone.

Oscar, *The Euterpeiad*, September 30, 1820

———

ON THE DEATH OF TWINS

ALAS, my BABES, how soon those eyes,
That us'd to sooth thy mother's woe,
Relentless death, that knows no ties,
Has seal'd them; and my babes laid low.

How did thy mother's feeble arms,
At first thee long for to embrace,
How pleas'd, I gaz'd upon your charms,
The image of your sire to trace.

But nipt those charms in early bud;
And in yon darksome house, the grave,
From my fond arms, mine eyes are hid,
The cypress o'er thee now does wave.

Sweet lovely babes, one joyous hour
Gave thee to life, and my fond arms;
So cruel death, in one, had power,
To blast my hopes, and hide these charms.

Yet sure 'twas heav'n's wise, highest, behest,
That call'd thee home, why should I mourn?
Farewell a while; sweet infants rest,
We'll meet in life's eternal morn.

D.M.L., *Universalist Magazine*, November 11, 1820

ACKNOWLEDGMENTS

This book would not exist without the support of Boston College administrators, faculty, students, and staff. As dean of the College of Arts and Sciences and then as provost and dean of faculties, David Quigley has promoted teaching about Boston across departments. Led by Mary Crane, the Institute for the Liberal Arts funded early, formative stages of this project. As English department chair, Suzanne Matson has championed undergraduate research collaborations, including this anthology. I have benefitted from discussions with colleagues who are engaged in teaching and writing about Boston, including Jeremiah McGrann, Scott Reznick, Carlo Rotella, and Owen Stanwood. From his base in O'Neill Library, Brendan Rapple provided regular assistance with online searches. Robert Stanton was always ready with advice about the meanings of old words and strategies for solving rebus clues. Eric Weiskott provided similar assistance with classical texts and languages. At crucial points in the project, John Anderson, Sophie Hagen, and Dennis Taylor read the full manuscript and provided much-appreciated encouragement. Christopher Boucher, George Hagen, Alan Richardson, James Wallace, Christopher P. Wilson, and Judith Wilt read parts of the manuscript. Alexandra Mitropoulos, a member of the research team, shared thoughtful readings and offered useful advice throughout the process. Treseanne K. Ainsworth, Judy Canty, Tracy Downing, Kristin Hartnett, and Linda Michel provided practical support. At the University Press of New England my editor, Richard Pult, was encouraging and supportive, Ann Brash guided the book through production with care, and Bronwyn Becker copyedited the manuscript masterfully. In the wider world of advocacy for Boston's literary heritage, I'm grateful for the collegiality of Peter Drummey, Jan Gardner, Susan Glover, Peter Jeffreys, Richard Kopley, Megan Marshall, Matthew Pearl, Philip E. Phillips, Elizabeth Prindle, Stefanie Rocknak, Jared Bowen, Andrea Shea, and the crew down at Grub Street. Librarians and archivists—notably Elizabeth Roscio at the Bostonian Society, Jane Winton and Tom Blake at the Boston Public Library, Jeanne Gamble at Historic New England, and Anna J. Clutterbuck-Cook at the Massachusetts Historical Society—helped with period images. Thanks are due to Wendy Lewis, Clara S. Lewis, Casey Sussman, and especially Marsden Lewis Sussman for support and encouragement. Finally, for the gifted students who participated in this project, the process—which included lively discussions and Eureka! moments—has been its own reward, while working with them has been the greatest pleasure of my professional life.

APPENDIX A

The number of poems published between 1789 and 1820 appears in parentheses

The Gentlemen and Ladies' Town and Country Magazine: Consisting of Literature, History, Politics, Arts, Manners, and Amusements, with Various Other Matter, 1789–90 (67)

The Massachusetts Magazine; or, Monthly Museum of Knowledge and Rational Entertainment, 1789–96 (654)

The American Apollo, 1792 (5)

The Tablet. A Miscellaneous Paper, Devoted to the Belles Lettres, 1795 (20)

The Nightingale, or, A Melange de Litterature; A Periodical Publication, 1796 (48)

The Columbian Phenix and Boston Review. Containing Useful Information on Literature, Religion, Morality, Politics and Philosophy; With Many Interesting Particulars in History and Biography, Forming a Compendium of the Present State of Society, 1800 (42)

The New England Quarterly Magazine; Comprehending Literature, Morals and Amusement, 1802 (40)

The Boston Weekly Magazine: Devoted to Morality, Literature, Biography, History, the Fine Arts, Agriculture, &c. &c., 1802–5 (242)

The Christian Observer, Conducted by Members of the Established Church, 1802–42 (43)

The Massachusetts Missionary Magazine, Containing Religious and Interesting Communications, Calculated to Edify Christians, and Inform the Rising Generation, 1803–8 (60)

The Monthly Anthology, and Boston Review, 1803–11 (223)

The Massachusetts Baptist Missionary Magazine, 1803–16 (35)

The Fly; or, Juvenile Miscellany, 1805–6 (20)

The Boston Magazine, 1805–6 (2)

The Literary Miscellany, Including Dissertations and Essays on Subjects of Literature, Science, and Morals; Biographical and Historical Sketches; Critical Remarks on Language; With Occasional Reviews, 1805–6 (7)

The Panoplist, 1805–8 (38)

The Polyanthos, 1805–14 (272)

Ladies Visitor, 1806 (1)

The Medical and Agricultural Register, For the Years 1806 and 1807, Containing Practical Information on Husbandry; Cautions and Directions For the Preservation of Health, Management of the Sick, &c., 1806–7 (3)

Ladies Afternoon Visitor, 1806–7 (29)

The Christian Monitor. Containing Prayers, Meditations, and Exercises; Designed for

the Use of Various Classes of Persons, and Particularly Young Heads of Families, 1806–11 (60)

The Emerald, or, Miscellany of Literature, 1806–8 (386)

The Thistle, 1807 (3)

The Panoplist and Missionary Magazine United, 1808–17 (6)

The Useful Cabinet, Published in Monthly Numbers for the New England Association of Inventors and Patrons of Useful Arts, 1808 (1)

The Witness; a Collection of Original and Selected Pieces on Various Religious Subjects, 1809 (4)

The Ordeal, 1809 (23)

Something, 1809–10 (45)

Omnium Gatherum, a Monthly Magazine, 1809–10 (15)

The Harvard Lyceum, 1810–11 (31)

The Scourge, 1811 (17)

The Juvenile Repository, 1811 (4)

The Cabinet; a Repository of Polite Literature, 1811 (17)

The Comet, 1811–12 (24)

The Satirist, January–April 1812 (19)

The Boston Satirist, or Weekly Museum, April–May 1812 (10)

The General Repository and Review, 1812–13 (12)

Christian Disciple, 1813–1818 (69)

The Boston Spectator; Devoted to Politicks and Belles-Lettres, 1814–15 (62)

The Friend of Peace, 1815–27 (10)

The North American Review and Miscellaneous Journal, 1815–21 (66)

The Recorder, 1816 (32)

The Boston Weekly Magazine, 1816–24 (240)

The Weekly Monitor, 1817 (10)

New-England Galaxy and Masonic Magazine, 1817–20 (368)

Boston Recorder, 1817–24 (202)

The American Baptist Magazine and Missionary Intelligencer, 1817–24 (17)

The Atheneum; or, Spirit of the English Magazines, 1817–33 (330)

The Panoplist, and Missionary Herald, 1818–20 (6)

The Christian Disciple and Theological Review, 1819–22 (6)

Christian Watchman, 1819–48 (106)

The Herald of Life and Immortality, 1819–20 (2)

The Universalist Magazine. Devoted to Doctrine, Religion, and Morality, 1819–20 (109)

The Club-Room, 1820 (2)

The Ladies' Port Folio, 1820 (58)

The Debtor's Journal, 1820–21 (3)

The Euterpeiad or, Musical Intelligencer, and Ladies Gazette, 1820–23 (66)

APPENDIX B

Representative Editorial Statements from the First Issues of Boston Magazines, 1789–1820

The Gentlemen and Ladies' Town and Country Magazine, February 1789

THE EDITOR of the *Gentlemen* and *Ladies Town* and *Country Magazine*, has the satisfaction to Address an indulgent Publick; more ready to commend, than censure: and flatters himself, that *Number One*, will meet with a favourable reception from the candid and liberal; although deficient of that intrinsic excellence, which lays a claim to merit.

To the maturing hand of experience—popular opinion—and friendly intercourse, all literary performances are highly indebted. From each of these sources the EDITOR hopes for improvement; and humbly sollicits every Son of Science, and Daughter of Genius, to favour him with their generous assistance, at the same moment begs leave to declare, that all communicated advice will be received with pleasure, considered impartially, and respectfully acknowledged.

The Ladies in particular, are earnestly entreated to patronize a Work, the major part of which, will ever be dedicated to their instruction, or amusement.

The Massachusetts Magazine, January 1789

TO THE PUBLICK: AGREEABLY to our promise, the MASSACHUSETTS MAGAZINE now makes its appearance—It has no *merit* that we can *boast of*—it is an *Infant*, but, under the fostering care of literary friends, may soon arrive to a respectful maturity.

Our best exertions shall not be wanting to render it worthy of the patronage we wish it to be favoured with, and which, should it fail of receiving, it must, like its *predecessors*, soon *cease to be*—but we are encouraged to hope that a work, which may be rendered so truly valuable, will not fail of being cultivated in a *soil* which *Genius* has marked for its own, and in which *literary Flowers* continually bud and blossom—let these Flowers only be handed to us—be transplanted into our parterre—and we shall soon be enabled to exhibit a most beautiful—a most useful variety.

The Tablet: A Miscellaneous Paper, Devoted to the Belles Lettres, May 19, 1795

Introductory Essay: We mean to offer, not to obtrude our sentiments; and though the scholar will discover little novelty in our remarks, yet the general class of readers may find in perusing them, something added to their amusement and something to their taste.

The Nightingale, or, A Melange de Litterature, May 10, 1796

Preface: We solicit the Public favor, and are sanguine in the expectation that a proof will now be given, that a literary periodical publication can be supported and encouraged in America. It has been suggested, that the inhabitants of Boston prefer viewing the manifest of a ship's cargo, to a lounge in the library. The business of a merchant is undoubtedly, highly honorable. The commercial interest of America, should ever be respected, and it is dignified by the conduct of those, who are engaged from principle and interest in its cause. But are there not hours when the mind requires amusement and relaxation? Are there not moments, when the intellectual faculties may, with profit and pleasure be indulged with a seclusion from the noise and bustle—with a tranquil retirement from the cares and anxieties of active life? Let it not be said, that in the pursuit of gain, Literature and the Muses are left at a distance, and that a sordid lust for gold has banished every noble sentiment, every mental delight from the bosoms of avaricious Bostonians. God forbid, that any foe to our country ever shall have reason to say, that our native town is the residence of Ignorance, tho' it should be the emporium of Plutus!

The Columbian Phenix and Boston Review, January 1800

To the Public: Aware that a publication of this kind cannot flourish long, without the assistance of able writers, the editor has endeavored . . . to make his Magazine the vehicle of a considerable share of original and useful communication. As the writers are to be known only by their works, it is by them alone, the public must judge of their merit and importance.

The Boston Weekly Magazine, October 30, 1802

GENERAL PLAN AND CONDITIONS of THIS PUBLICATION. THE Editors and Proprietors of the Boston Weekly Magazine, respectfully present the public, with this sheet, as the Specimen of a Work, both in matter and manner, which they have been induced to commence, at the recommendation of their friends. . . .

In furnishing *original* matter, (and from the quantity this day presented, we may expect much) we must depend on the friendship of those who have the ability, and disposition to oblige us with the fruits of their genius and erudition—we hope to experience a portion of such friendship; and trust we shall not be found undeserving of it.

The Monthly Anthology and Boston Review, November 1, 1803

The Loiterer—No. 1: The hills and vallies, variegated with bright villages, fruit-ful fields and pleasant groves [of the United States], display prospects, that far sur-pass the most lively visions of fancy. These wild and elegant landscapes loudly invoke the imitative powers of the painter. Poetry, the lovely nurse of virtue and taste, if wooed with that ardent assiduity, which her exalted dignity requires, would surely delight in this alluring residence. . . .

Genius has sometimes dawned among us, but its opening brilliancy has been too often and too suddenly obscured by the gloom of neglect. But whence arises this neglect? Does it come from a prejudice against our own talents, from insen-sibility of taste, or from an envious disposition to silence the voice of fame? Or must we assign it to the predominant sway of avarice? In particular instances all these may induce neglect; but perhaps the principal cause is the want of zealous perseverance in the candidates for literary distinction. They, who have opportu-nity and genius, too frequently pass their time in apathy and indolence, in roving some barren field of pleasure, or else, as is most frequently the case, engage in our common pursuit of fortune. So few are they, who engage themselves wholly in the study of literature and in speculating on life and manners, that the design of their occupation is very little understood. . . . Those, who may incline to co-operate in this undertaking, are cordially invited to contribute their assistance.

The Fly; or Juvenile Miscellany, October 16, 1805

To the Public: . . . it will be the undeviating aim of the Editors, to present a valu-able combination of useful and interesting subjects, particularly designed for the improvement of YOUTH of both sexes. They pledge themselves that in their work will never be found a sentiment inimical to religion, morality, virtue or delicacy; but such harmless productions only, (original and selected) as will at once in-struct and amuse. It will be agreeably diversified with subjects humorous, literary and light—Essays instructive and amusing, Historical and Biographical sketches, Poetry, Tales, Epigrams, Anecdotes, and a variety of incidental matter. They in-tend that theirs, like other *Flies*, shall *at least* be harmless, and they dare promise, that with the proffered assistance of their literary friends, it will be an amusing and instructive companion for a winter's evening fire-side.

Under these impressions, they now take leave of their readers, referring the work, and the annexed conditions, to a candid and generous public; with a hope that the fly, while carefully alighting only on the sweets of literature, and culling for the intellectual bower the choicest delicacies, may be sustained by the sun-shine of favour, and nourished by the encouraging patronage of the YOUTH of *Boston* . . . to whose service it will be devoted, and is respectfully dedicated, by *THE EDITORS.*

The Ordeal, January 7, 1809

GENERAL INTRODUCTION: Though the editors are completely sensible of the difficulties they must be obliged to encounter in their struggle for success, and though it is their lot to have fallen upon times pregnant with corruptions in politicks, religion and literature, but barren alike of patriotism, and munificence; yet, supported by their confidence in the sterling merit of *old fashioned* principles, they do not shrink from their attempt; and even should it prove abortive, they can compromise with misfortune from the impression that they have intended well, and have offered some feeble aid to that glorious opposition which has for its object the attainment of peace without dishonour, government without experiment, and national energy without national disgrace. We wish our political, religious and literary sentiments to be unequivocally understood, and our intentions openly explained: We think the political errours of the times fatal to the best interests of the community, and that such principles of religion and literature are spreading abroad as are calculated vitally to injure our national establishments. The paramount necessity of securing our civil and political existence should unite all honest men in an ardent effort to exhibit to the view *of the people* the deformities which disgrace the present administration of government, by tearing away the curtain of hypocrisy under which they have long been concealed.

Harvard Lyceum, July 14, 1810

ADDRESS OF THE EDITORS. IN pursuance of the Prospectus, presented to the publick about two months ago, the first number of the HARVARD LYCEUM now makes its appearance. As we must look to the publick for the patronage, necessary to uphold our paper . . . [it] is surely an unnecessary task to argue the utility of a literary journal. The extensive encouragement ever afforded to such as have deserved it, sufficiently shows, that, in the estimation of the world, a good magazine of literature is a good thing. If the name has been abused, and employed as the herald of nonsense and ignorance, it is something to the credit of its popularity, that it has had the authority to recommend them to publick notice . . . we assure our subscribers that a part of every number shall be unalienably devoted with religious sacredness to original poetry. Poetry we call it, it shall be verse: and what more do you expect in a newspaper ode?

The Cabinet, January 5, 1811

ADVERTISEMENT. To the question, "why is another publication announced in Boston, where cold neglect has so frequently chilled the ardour of literary ambition?" the publisher of the Cabinet will offer no prolix replication. Modest assurance is never more embarrassed than in soliciting the attention of the public to a work, the character of which is wholly comprised in anticipations and futurities. Not wishing to surprise confidence by magnificent promises easy to make but always difficult to fulfill, the publisher will merely express his full persuasion that the gentlemen who have undertaken to conduct this literary miscellany will not disappoint the expectation he has formed of establishing a publication which shall merit public patronage.

The Scourge, August 10, 1811

ADDRESS. The EDITOR begs leave to introduce his Scourge to a discerning and patriotic Public; with a hope that it will be found, even in its first efforts, to do much good, and deserve liberal support. . . . The political situation of this countrye and of this commonwealth in particular; the conduct of our national and state rulers; and the lies and intrigues of our leading democrats—will form the principal subjects of the Scourge—and, as with energy was observed by a celebrated writer,

"What I know to be true, that will I declare; and what I feel to be my duty to represent, that will I have the boldness to publish."

The Editor anticipates much assistance from able pens in enabling him to expose, to merited ridicule and contempt, the wicked, and but too often successful arts, of our leading democrats.

TIM TOUCHSTONE

The Comet, October 19, 1811

READER! Before you find fault with the frontispiece and title we have chosen, give us time to say, that we think our work, in many of its essential properties, bears a striking resemblance to the celestial comet, now visible in our hemisphere, and therefore appropriate. If, in the style of a conundrum maker, you ask, Why? we answer,

First. Because it will *move in a very eccentrick orbit.* Its motions will be irregular, sometimes *direct*, sometimes *retrograde.*

Secondly. It will puzzle the heads of many great philosophers to find out its *component elements*, and for what purpose it visits OUR SYSTEM.

Thirdly. It is expected that a *train of light* will follow it, which will be *brightest immediately after the perihelion.*

Fourthly. We hope it will resemble our celestial visitor by soon getting into *the circle of perpetual apparition*, and passing through all the *constellations of the zodiack* of fashion and taste.

Fifthly. Reasoning from experience and analogy, it will, in all probability, soon *pass off into the regions of space* and become *invisible.*

But, READER! we hope it will never resemble any celestial comet, either by *producing a deluge*, or *setting the world on fire.*

The Boston Satirist, April 20, 1812

The public may rest assured that neither the tongue of a slanderer nor the assaults of a low-bred scoundrel, will ever deter the editor from exposing to public view those pests of society, who think they have the exclusive privilege of traducing the characters of their superiors.

The Christian Watchman, May 29, 1819

PROSPECTUS. The object of this paper will be to present to the public, the most important religious intelligence of every kind, contained in the various publications of the present day. Its pages will be filled with the Reports of Bible, Missionary and Tract Societies, both in this and in other countries; with accounts of Revivals of Religion, the Constitution of Churches, the Ordination of Ministers, and in general whatever relates to the prosperity of the Redeemer's Kingdom. . . .

But why publish a new paper? . . .

In this great and growing metropolis, *only one* paper is published of a religious character, while the number of the political and miscellaneous kind, exceeds a dozen. Only *four* religious papers are published in the whole New-England. Can it be supposed that *politics* will continue to occupy, almost exclusively, the labors of the press? Are politics the supreme concern of man? Ought they to usurp the greatest share of public and private attention? The time of political wonder has gone by. A new and most blessed era has commenced; an era of religious triumph. The *tidings of destruction* having it is to be hoped, nearly come to an end, christians now have leisure to attend to the *tidings of salvation*. They must, they will enquire after the great things which God is doing in the world. Religious newspapers must and will continue to multiply. The number yet is much too small for the demand. Not one fifth part of the community is yet supplied with them.

Ladies' Port Folio, January 1, 1820

To the patrons of the LADIES' PORT FOLIO.

In commencing a periodical work, it is usual to make high sounding pretensions, and to arrogate a superiority of advantages; without considering the character of other journals, or the means necessary for its accomplishment . . . our present object is not to show the merits and defects of others, but to talk of our own affairs, to speak of ourselves as we are; inexperienced, a mere cock-boat, and to borrow the language of a famous dashing fourth of July orator in the vicinity of Bunker's Hill, "without chart or compass," and almost "without object or destination," except to please the ladies; and "liable to founder in the mountain waves of commotion, to perish in the *intellectual* storm, or to shipwreck in the fluctuations of the veering gale." Sufficiently flattering will be our efforts, if we receive a portion of that patronage with which our competitors are deservedly honoured;

and sufficiently able shall we conceive ourselves if we can follow at no humble distance, in the pathway which has led *them* to fame.

. . . Though originally intended for the amusement of the other sex, there can be no fear that it will be equally fitted to the capacities of our own; and we hope it will not fail to be interesting to both. If either are disposed to contribute a portion of their literary wealth in its encouragement, it will be most thankfully received; and with this impression, that nothing will emanate from the one, which on the ground of delicacy or intelligence, the other would blush to read. As that morality is the most useful, which is inculcated in an entertaining mode, and those relations the best adapted for perusal, the foundation of which are derived from real life, it is anticipated that our correspondents (if we are so fortunate as to have any,) will render such a course the leading principle of their compositions.

BIBLIOGRAPHY

Suggested Reading on Magazines, Literature, Culture, and Life in the United States in General and Boston in Particular, 1789–1820

Boydston, Jeanne. *Home and Work: Housework, Wages, and the Ideology of Labor in the Early Republic*. New York: Oxford University Press, 1990.

Branson, Susan. *Dangerous to Know: Women, Crime, and Notoriety in the Early Republic*. Philadelphia: University of Pennsylvania Press, 2008.

Burgett, Bruce. *Sentimental Bodies: Sex, Gender, and Citizenship in the Early Republic*. Princeton, NJ: Princeton University Press, 1998.

Chielens, Edward E. *American Literary Magazines: The Eighteenth and Nineteenth Centuries*. New York: Greenwood Press, 1986.

Cotlar, Seth. *Tom Paine's America: The Rise and Fall of Transatlantic Radicalism in the Early Republic*. Charlottesville: University of Virginia Press, 2011.

Crawford, Mary Caroline. *Old Boston Days and Ways: From the Dawn of the Revolution until the Town Became a City*. Boston: Little, Brown, 1909.

Davidson, Cathy N. *Revolution and the Word: The Rise of the Novel in America*. New York: Oxford University Press, 1986; 2004.

Edgar, Neal A. *History and Bibliography of American Magazines, 1810–1820*. Metuchen, NJ: Scarecrow Press, 1975.

Elliott, Emory. *American Writers of the Early Republic*. Detroit: Gale Research Co., 1985.

Ferguson, Robert A. *Reading the Early Republic*. Cambridge, MA: Harvard University Press, 2004.

Fliegelman, Jay. *Prodigals and Pilgrims: The American Revolution against Patriarchal Authority, 1750–1800*. Cambridge, MA: Cambridge University Press, 1982.

Gardner, Jared. *The Rise and Fall of Early American Magazine Culture*. Chicago: University of Illinois Press, 2012.

Gilmore, Michael T. "The Literature of the Revolutionary and Early National Periods," in *The Cambridge History of American Literature*, vol. 1: 1590–1820, 539–694. Edited by Sacvan Bercovitch. Cambridge, MA: Cambridge University Press, 1994; 2008.

Graham, Maryemma, and Jerry W. Ward, Jr., eds. *The Cambridge History of African American Literature*. Cambridge, MA: Cambridge University Press, 2011.

Green, Martin. *The Problem of Boston: Some Readings in Cultural History*. New York: W. W. Norton, 1966.

Gross, Robert A., and Mary Kelley, eds. *An Extensive Republic: Print, Culture, and Society in the New Nation, 1790–1840*, vol. 2 in *A History of the Book in America*. Chapel Hill: University of North Carolina Press, 2010.

Kann, Mark E. *Taming Passion for the Public Good: Policing Sex in the Early Republic*. New York: New York University Press, 2012.

Kaplan, Catherine O'Donnell. *Men of Letters in the Early Republic: Cultivating Forums of Citizenship*. Chapel Hill: University of North Carolina Press, 2008.

Kitch, Carolyn L. *Pages from the Past: History and Memory in American Magazines.* Chapel Hill: University of North Carolina Press, 2005.

Lewis, Paul, curator. *Forgotten Chapters of Boston's Literary History.* www.bostonliteraryhistory.com.

Mott, Frank Luther. *A History of American Magazines, 1741–1850.* Cambridge, MA: Harvard University Press, 1957.

Laderman, Gary. *The Sacred Remains: American Attitudes toward Death, 1799–1883.* New Haven, CT: Yale University Press, c1996.

McGill, Meredith L., ed. *The Traffic in Poems: Nineteenth-Century Poetry and Transatlantic Exchange.* New Brunswick: Rutgers University Press, 2008.

Nathans, Heather S. *Early American Theatre from the Revolution to Thomas Jefferson: Into the Hands of the People.* Cambridge, MA: Cambridge University Press, 2003.

O'Connell, Shaun. *Imagining Boston: A Literary Landscape.* Boston: Beacon Press, 1990.

Price, Kenneth, and Susan Belasco Smith, eds. *Periodical Literature in Nineteenth-Century America.* Charlottesville: University of Virginia Press, 1995.

Richardson, Lyon N. *A History of Early American Magazines.* New York: Thomas Nelson and Sons, 1931.

Roth, Marjorie K. *The Book of Boston: The Federal Period, 1775–1837.* New York: Hastings House Publisher, 1961.

Sharp, James Roger. *American Politics in the Early Republic: The New Nation in Crisis.* New Haven, CT: Yale University Press, 1993.

Shields, David. S., ed. *American Poetry: The Seventeenth and Eighteenth Centuries.* New York: Library of America, 2007.

Snow, Caleb H. *History of Boston.* Boston: A. Bowen, 1825.

Stark, James Henry. *Stark's Antique Views of Boston.* Boston: James H. Stark, 1901.

Travers, Len. *Celebrating the Fourth: Independence Day and the Rites of Nationalism in the Early Republic.* Amherst: University of Massachusetts Press, 1997.

Warner, Michael. *The Letters of the Republic: Publication and the Public Sphere in Eighteenth-Century America.* Cambridge, MA: Harvard University Press, 1992.

Wilson, Susan (for the Boston History Collaborative). *The Literary Trail of Greater Boston.* Beverly, MA: Commonwealth Editions, 2005.

Wood, Gordon S. *Empire of Liberty: A History of the Early Republic, 1789–1815.* New York: Oxford University Press, 2011.

Zboray, Ronald J. *A Fictive People: Antebellum Economic Development and the American Reading Public.* New York: Oxford University Press, 1993.